1000 words
Level 4

西厢记
Romance of the West Chamber

王帅 改编　张乐 翻译

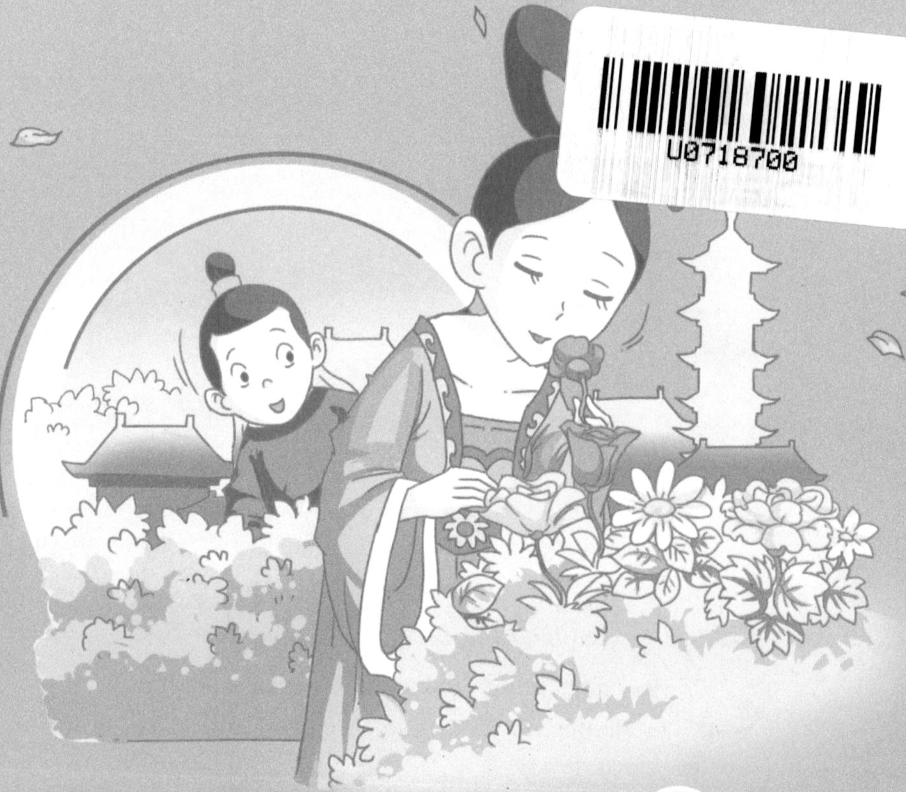

MP3
Download Online

First Edition   2017
Third Printing   2023

ISBN 978-7-5138-1246-7
Copyright 2017 by Sinolingua Co., Ltd
Published by Sinolingua Co., Ltd
24 Baiwanzhuang Street, Beijing 100037, China
Tel: (86) 10-68320585   68997826
Fax: (86) 10-68997826   68326333
http://www.sinolingua.com.cn
E-mail: hyjx@sinolingua.com.cn
Printed by Beijing Hucais Culture Communication Co., Ltd

Printed in the People's Republic of China

编者的话

对于广大汉语学习者来说，要想快速提高汉语水平，扩大阅读量是很有必要的。"彩虹桥"汉语分级读物为汉语学习者提供了一系列有趣、有用的汉语阅读材料。本系列读物按照词汇量进行分级，力求用限定的词汇讲述精彩的故事。本套读物主要有以下特点：

一、**分级精准，循序渐进**。我们参考"新汉语水平考试（HSK）词汇表"（2012年修订版）、《汉语国际教育用音节汉字词汇等级划分（国家标准）》和《常用汉语1500高频词语表》等词汇分级标准，结合《欧洲语言教学与评估框架性共同标准》（CEFR），设计了一套适合汉语学习者的"彩虹桥"词汇分级标准。本系列读物分为7个级别（入门级*、1级、2级、3级、4级、5级、6级），供不同水平的汉语学习者选择，每个级别故事的生词数量不超过本级别对应词汇量的20%。随着级别的升高，故事的篇幅逐渐加长。本系列读物与HSK、CEFR的对应级别，各级词汇量以及每本书的字数详见下表。

---

* 入门级（Starter）在封底用S标识。

级别	入门级	1级	2级	3级	4级	5级	6级
对应级别	HSK1 CEFR A1	HSK1-2 CEFR A1-A2	HSK2-3 CEFR A2-B1	HSK3 CEFR A2-B1	HSK3-4 CEFR B1	HSK4 CEFR B1-B2	HSK5 CEFR B2-C1
词汇量	150	300	500	750	1 000	1 500	2 500
字数	1 000	2 500	5 000	7 500	10 000	15 000	25 000

二、**故事精彩，题材多样**。本套读物选材的标准就是"精彩"，所选的故事要么曲折离奇，要么感人至深，对读者构成奇妙的吸引力。选题广泛取材于中国的神话传说、民间故事、文学名著、名人传记和历史故事等，让汉语学习者在阅读中潜移默化地了解中国的文化和历史。

三、**结构合理，实用性强**。"彩虹桥"系列读物的每一本书中，除了中文故事正文之外，都配有主要人物的中英文介绍、生词英文注释及例句、故事正文的英文翻译、练习题和生词表，方便读者阅读和理解故事内容，提升汉语阅读能力。练习题主要采用客观题，题型多样，难度适中，并附有参考答案，既可供汉语教师在课堂上教学使用，又可供汉语学习者进行自我水平检测。

如果您对本系列读物有什么想法，比如推荐精彩故事、提出改进意见等，请发邮件到 liuxiaolin@sinolingua.com.cn，与我们交流探讨。也可以关注我们的微信公众号 CHQRainbowBridge，随时与我们交流互动。同时，微信公众号会不定期发布有关"彩虹桥"的出版信息，以及汉语阅读、中国文化小知识等。

韩 颖 刘小琳

Preface

For students who study Chinese as a foreign language, it's crucial for them to enlarge the scope of their reading to improve their comprehension skills. The "Rainbow Bridge" Graded Chinese Reader series is designed to provide a collection of interesting and useful Chinese reading materials. This series grades each volume by its vocabulary level and brings the learners into every scene through vivid storytelling. The series has the following features:

I. A gradual approach by grading the volumes based on vocabulary levels. We have consulted the New HSK Vocabulary (2012 Revised Edition), the *Graded Chinese Syllables, Characters and Words for the Application of Teaching Chinese to the Speakers of Other Languages (National Standard)* and the 1500 Commonly Used High Frequency Chinese Vocabulary, along with the Common European Framework of Reference for Languages (CEFR) to design the "Rainbow Bridge" vocabulary grading standard. The series is divided into seven levels (Starter*, Level 1, Level 2, Level 3, Level 4, Level 5 and Level 6) for students at different stages in their Chinese education to choose from. For each level, new words are no more than 20% of the vocabulary amount as specified in the corresponding HSK and CEFR levels. As the levels progress, the passage length will in turn increase. The following table indicates the corresponding "Rainbow Bridge" level, HSK and CEFR levels, the vocabulary amount, and number of characters.

---

* Represented by "S" on the back cover.

Level	Starter	1	2	3	4	5	6
HSK/ CEFR Level	HSK1 CEFR A1	HSK1-2 CEFR A1-A2	HSK2-3 CEFR A2-B1	HSK3 CEFR A2-B1	HSK3-4 CEFR B1	HSK4 CEFR B1-B2	HSK5 CEFR B2-C1
Vocabulary	150	300	500	750	1,000	1,500	2,500
Characters	1,000	2,500	5,000	7,500	10,000	15,000	25,000

II. Intriguing stories on various themes. The series features engaging stories known for their twists and turns as well as deeply touching plots. The readers will find it a joyful experience to read the stories. The topics are selected from Chinese mythology, legends, folklore, literary classics, biographies of renowned people and historical tales. Such wide-ranging topics exert an invisible, yet formative, influence on readers' understanding of Chinese culture and history.

III. Reasonably structured and easy to use. For each volume of the "Rainbow Bridge" series, apart from a Chinese story, we also provide an introduction to the main characters in Chinese and English, new words with English explanations and sample sentences, and an English translation of the story, followed by comprehension exercises and a vocabulary list to help users read and understand the story and improve their Chinese reading skills. The exercises are mainly presented as objective questions that take on various forms with moderate difficulty. Moreover, keys to the exercises are also provided. The series can be used by teachers in class or by students for self-study.

If you have any questions, comments or suggestions about the series, please email us at liuxiaolin@sinolingua.com.cn. You can also exchange ideas with us via our WeChat account: CHQRainbowBridge. This account will provide updates on the series along with Chinese reading materials and cultural tips.

Han Ying and Liu Xiaolin

目　　录
Contents

一、张生初见崔莺莺……………………………… 1

二、花园对诗，殿上偷看………………………… 7

三、莺莺遇险，张生退兵………………………… 14

四、老夫人请客，夫妻变兄妹…………………… 21

五、莺莺夜听琴…………………………………… 29

六、红娘传情书…………………………………… 34

七、张生猜谜语…………………………………… 40

八、莺莺张生月夜相会…………………………… 47

九、老夫人同意婚事，张生进京考试…………… 53

十、有情人终成眷属……………………………… 59

English Version……………………………………… 68

练习题………………………………………………… 95

练习题答案…………………………………………… 100

词汇表………………………………………………… 101

主要人物和地点：
Main Characters and Places

张生（Zhāng Shēng）：唐朝的一个读书人。
Zhang Sheng: A scholar living during the Tang Dynasty (618—907).

崔莺莺（Cuī Yīngying）：崔相国的女儿，非常美丽。
Cui Yingying: The beautiful daughter of the Counselor-in-Chief.

红娘（Hóngniáng）：崔莺莺的丫鬟。
Hongniang: The maid of Cui Yingying.

老夫人（lǎofūren）：崔莺莺的母亲。
Madam Cui: Cui Yingying's mother.

长老（zhǎnglǎo）：普救寺里地位最高的和尚。
The elder: The monk of greater authority in Pujiu Monastery.

杜确（Dù Què）：张生的朋友，人称"白马将军"。
Du Que: Zhang Sheng's friend, also known by the name "General White Horse."

郑恒（Zhèng Héng）：老夫人的侄子。
Zheng Heng: The nephew of Madam Cui.

长安（Cháng'ān）：中国唐代的首都，现在的陕西省西安市。
Chang'an: Present-day Xi'an in Shaanxi Province, the capital of China during the Tang Dynasty.

河中府（Hézhōng Fǔ）：唐代地名，现在的山西省永济县蒲州镇。
Hezhong Prefecture: A place during the Tang Dynasty in present-day Puzhou Town, Yongji County, Shanxi Province.

普救寺（Pǔjiù Sì）：位于山西省永济县的一座佛寺。
Pujiu Monastery: A monastery located in Yongji County, Shanxi Province.

中文故事

西厢①记

一、张生初见崔莺莺

唐朝②时有个读书人名叫张生，他要去京城③长安参加科举④考试。他路过一个叫河中府的地方，这个地方有一座有名的寺庙⑤叫普救寺。张生决定去参观一下。

在普救寺里，张生这里看看，那里看看，走到一个小花园⑥，突然发现一位姑娘正在摘⑦花。

① 西厢 (xīxiāng) n.
west chamber
e.g., 莺莺住在西厢房。

② 唐朝 (Tángcháo) n. the Tang Dynasty (618-907)
e.g., 唐朝是中国古代的一个朝代。

③ 京城 (jīngchéng) n. capital (of a country)
e.g., 西安是唐朝的京城。

④ 科举 (kējǔ) n. imperial civil examination
e.g., 中国古代用科举考试选拔官员。

⑤ 寺庙 (sìmiào) n. temple, monastery
e.g., 这座山上有很多寺庙。

⑥ 花园 (huāyuán) n. garden
e.g., 花园里有很多漂亮的花。

⑦ 摘 (zhāi) v. pluck, pick
e.g., 她从树上摘了一个苹果。

这位姑娘看起来十八九岁，长得非常漂亮。张生吃了一惊①，心想："世界上怎么会有这么美丽的姑娘？难道是天上的仙女②？"这时又来了一个丫鬟③打扮的小姑娘，也非常漂亮。但是一转眼，两位姑娘都离开了花园。

张生赶紧找到寺庙里的小和尚④，问："你们的花园里有仙女，是吗？"小和尚奇怪地说："哪里有什么仙女？"张生又问："花园里那个摘花的姑娘，不是仙女吗？"小和尚笑了，"不是仙女，那位小姐姓崔，名叫莺莺，是崔相国⑤的

① 吃惊 (chījīng) v. be surprised
e.g., 看到来了这么多人，他吃了一惊。

② 仙女 (xiānnǚ) n. fairy
e.g., 她长得非常漂亮，像天上的仙女一样。

③ 丫鬟 (yāhuan) n. maid
e.g., 红娘是崔莺莺的丫鬟。

④ 和尚 (héshang) n. Buddhist monk
e.g., 和尚不能结婚。

⑤ 相国 (xiàngguó) n. Counselor-in-Chief
e.g., 相国相当于现在的总理。

① 去世 (qùshì) *v.*
pass away
e.g., 莺莺的父亲去世了，她很难过。

② 灵柩 (língjiù) *n.*
coffin
e.g., 父亲去世以后，他带着父亲的灵柩回到家乡。

女儿。她的父亲去世①了，她妈妈和她带着父亲的灵柩②回家乡，因为有事要在这里住一段时间。"张生接着问："那另外一个姑娘是谁？"小和尚说："哦，那是崔小姐的丫鬟，名叫红娘。"

晚上，张生怎么也睡不着，总是想着那个姑娘的样子。他一遍又一遍念着"崔莺莺"这个名字。"没想到在这里会遇到这么美丽的姑娘，要是我能和她在一起该多好啊！我一定要认识她。她的丫鬟会帮助我吗？不管怎么样，为了她，我也要在这个寺庙住下！"张生做了这个决定，才慢慢睡着了。

第二天，张生就去见

寺庙的长老①，他送给长老一两银子作为房租②，要求住在这里。长老说："我们这里有很多空房间，你可以住下。"正在说话的时候，一个小姑娘进来找长老，她问："长老，我们夫人问您什么时候可以给崔相国做法事③。"张生抬头一看，说话的正是那个叫红娘的丫

① 长老 (zhǎnglǎo) n. elder
e.g., 寺庙的长老年纪很大。

② 房租 (fángzū) n. rent
e.g., 这个城市的房租很贵。

③ 法事 (fǎshì) n. religious service
e.g., 这些和尚会为死去的人做法事。

① 尴尬 (gāngà) *adj.* awkward, embarrassed
e.g., 两个人第一次见面没话说，很尴尬。

鬟。长老回答："这个月的十五日就可以了。"

红娘刚走出长老的房间，张生赶紧走上前去打招呼："姑娘你好！"红娘礼貌地回答："先生您好，有事吗？"张生说："请问你是不是莺莺小姐的丫鬟？"红娘回答："是啊，先生您是哪位？"张生激动地说："啊啊，我叫张生，今年二十三岁，我的生日是一月十七号，我还没有结婚……""谁问你结没结婚了！"红娘又气又笑地说。张生很尴尬①，赶紧解释："我是想问莺莺小姐常出来玩吗？"红娘一听就生气了，说："看你也是个读书人，怎么会这么不懂礼貌，'<u>男女授受不亲</u>①'你不懂吗？你怎么可以随便打听没结婚姑娘的情况呢？以后该问的问，不该问的别<u>瞎</u>②问！"说完，<u>红娘</u>头也不回就走了。看着红娘生气的<u>背影</u>③，<u>张生</u>感到很后悔，"看来这个丫鬟不好<u>惹</u>④。怎么样才能接近莺莺呢？我得好好想一想。"

男女授受不亲
(nánnǚ shòushòu bù qīn)
Men and women should keep a proper distance from each other. This was the norm in ancient China. It was forbidden for men and women to have any body contact or conversations or to pass things to each other.
e.g., 中国古代男女授受不亲，未婚女子不能随便跟男人讲话。

② 瞎 (xiā) adv. foolishly, blindly, groundlessly
e.g., 你不知道就不要瞎说。

③ 背影 (bèiyǐng) n. figure
e.g., 他送一个朋友，一直到背影也看不见了。

④ 惹 (rě) v. cause, offend
e.g., 他经常惹父母生气。

二、花园对诗，殿上偷看

红娘回来跟老夫人讲了做法事的事，然后来到小姐的西厢房，对莺莺说："姐姐，跟你讲一件好玩的事。今天我在寺庙里遇到一个特别有意思的读书人。"然后她就把遇到张生的事情讲给莺莺听。莺莺听了也觉得很好笑，对红娘说："这件事千万别告诉老夫人。天晚了，咱们去花园烧香①吧。"

花园里月光如水，莺莺点上香开始祷告②："第一炷③香，祝我的父亲早进天界④；第二炷香，祝我的母亲平安健康；第三炷香……"莺莺没有继续说。红娘抢⑤过来说："这一炷

---

① 烧香 (shāoxiāng) *v.* burn incense
e.g., 他经常到寺庙烧香。

② 祷告 (dǎogào) *v.* pray
e.g., 她一边烧香一边祷告。

③ 炷 (zhù) *m.w.* (for sticks of incense)
e.g., 在佛前上一炷香。

④ 天界 (tiānjiè) *n.* realm of heaven
e.g., 很多人相信人死了以后会到天界。

⑤ 抢 (qiǎng) *v.* rush to
e.g., 我还没说话，他就抢着说了起来。

香，祝莺莺姐姐找一个好姐夫①。"莺莺没有说话，深深地叹了一口气②。

正在这时，突然墙③外面传④来一个男人念诗⑤的声音，"月光照夜明，花儿多安静，月亮如此近，不见月中人？"[1] 红娘赶紧⑥说："小姐，你听！这声音好像就是那个二十三岁还

① 姐夫 (jiěfu) n. brother-in-law (elder sister's husband)
e.g., 姐姐的丈夫叫姐夫。

② 叹气 (tànqì) v. sigh
e.g., 他心里难过，叹了一口气。

③ 墙 (qiáng) n. wall
e.g., 院子里的墙很高。

④ 传 (chuán) v. pass, transmit
e.g., 远处传来了好听的歌声。

⑤ 诗 (shī) n. poem
e.g., 离开中国的时候，他写了一首诗。

⑥ 赶紧 (gǎnjǐn) adv. hurriedly, hastily
e.g., 快上课了，他赶紧往学校跑。

① 傻瓜 (shǎguā) *n.*
fool
e.g., 这么好的工作他不去，别人都说他是傻瓜。

② 特意 (tèyì) *adv.*
on purpose
e.g., 过生日的那天，她特意穿了一件漂亮的衣服。

③ 藏 (cáng) *v.* hide
e.g., 这个孩子把自己的苹果藏了起来。

④ 角落 (jiǎoluò) *n.*
corner
e.g., 他坐在房间的角落，很多人没看到他。

没有结婚的傻瓜①。"

原来小和尚告诉张生莺莺每天都会来花园烧香，于是他特意②藏③在花园的一个角落④等着。听到莺莺的祷告，张生心想："原来莺莺也在向往爱情。是不是对我有意思呢？我赶紧做一首诗念给她听。"于是他做了一首诗大声地念出来。

听到张生的诗，莺莺觉得水平很高："好诗好诗！我也照着做一首给他。"于是莺莺也做了一首诗念了出来，"独自在房间，寂寞又孤单，那边吟诗人，你应知我心。[2]"。听到莺莺的回应，张生吃了一惊，"这莺莺小姐对得这么快这么好，真是又漂亮又有才华①！我得马上过去和她见面。"

张生从角落出来，满脸带笑来到莺莺面前。莺莺见到张生出来，也不吃惊，刚要说话，红娘却说："小姐，有人来了，咱们快走，省得老夫人发脾气。"莺莺也不说话，转身和红娘往房间走去。张生心里一沉②："唉，这个红娘怎么这样呢？太不配合了。"张生失望地准备回房间，突然听到"哗啦啦③"的声音。"难道莺莺又回来找我了？"张生赶紧转身④回头看，但哪里有莺莺和红娘呢，原来是一只鸟从花丛⑤里飞到天上。"唉，我的命

① 才华 (cáihuá) n. talent
e.g., 这个年轻人很有才华。

② 沉 (chén) v. sink, plummet
e.g., 听到这个不好的消息，他心里一沉。

③ 哗啦啦 (huālālā) onom. crash, rustle
e.g., 小河流水哗啦啦响。

④ 转身 (zhuǎnshēn) v. turn around
e.g., 他生气了，转身回家了。

⑤ 花丛 (huācóng) n. flowers in clusters
e.g., 小狗在花丛里跑。

① 大殿 (dàdiàn) *n.* hall
e.g., 大殿是寺庙里最大的房间。

② 念经 (niànjīng) *v.* chant Buddhist scriptures
e.g., 做法事的时候，和尚要念经。

③ 寻找 (xúnzhǎo) *v.* look for
e.g., 他的孩子不见了，大家到处去寻找。

④ 偷偷 (tōutōu) *adv.* stealthily
e.g., 他偷偷从家里跑了出来。

⑤ 盯 (dīng) *v.* stare at
e.g., 这个孩子一直盯着我手里的水果。

⑥ 眼泪 (yǎnlèi) *n.* tear
e.g., 她流下了眼泪。

⑦ 入迷 (rùmí) *v.* be fascinated, be lost in
e.g., 他看这本书入了迷，忘了吃饭。

⑧ 灭 (miè) *v.* go out
e.g., 灯灭了，房间一下子黑了。

怎么这么苦呢！今天肯定睡不着了。"

听说莺莺的母亲要为去世的崔相国办法事，张生赶紧去找长老，想参加这场法事，长老同意了。

到了办法事的这一天，张生一大早就来到寺庙的大殿①，看到大殿里非常热闹，和尚们都在念经②。他到处寻找③莺莺，发现老夫人带着莺莺和红娘坐在前面，莺莺正在哭自己的父亲。张生一边干活，一边偷偷④地盯⑤着莺莺看。只见莺莺脸上挂着眼泪⑥，像带雨的花一样美丽。张生在那边看得入了迷⑦，长老赶紧提醒他："张生，那边的灯灭⑧了，快去点灯。"张生不好意思再看，低着头去点灯。

莺莺听到长老说话，也看到了张生，心想："这个读书人长得真帅气①，而且又那么有才华，他这么走来走去是为了接近我吧。"红娘小声对莺莺说："小姐，你看那个张生，我猜他昨天一夜②没睡好，就

① 帅气 (shuàiqì) *adj.* handsome
e.g., 那个男孩长得很帅气，很多女孩喜欢他。

② 夜 (yè) *n.* night
e.g., 他一夜都没有睡觉。

① 亮 (liàng) *v.* shine, lighten
e.g., 天亮了，太阳出来了。

② 假装 (jiǎzhuāng) *v.* pretend
e.g., 他假装生气，不和别人说话。

③ 舍不得 (shěbude) *v.* loathe to part with
e.g., 那件衣服很漂亮，但他舍不得花钱买。

等着天亮①来看你呢。"莺莺假装②生气，"别乱说！"

张生发现莺莺和红娘在看自己，非常高兴，心里说："莺莺，我对你的爱你能感觉到吗？"这时候，长老站起来说："法事结束了，请老夫人和小姐回房间。""这么快就结束了？"张生还没看够莺莺，非常舍不得③地离开了大殿。

"唉，什么时候才能再见到莺莺呢？怎么才能和她认识呢？"张生又睡不着了。

三、莺莺遇险，张生退兵

当张生正在发愁①怎么和莺莺更进一步的时候，寺庙出事了。

一个叫孙飞虎的将军②造反③，到处杀人放火，抢劫④老百姓。他听说崔相国的女儿非常漂亮，想抢来做自己的妻子，于是派⑤了军队⑥包围了寺庙，要求长老三天之内把莺莺交给他，否则就把寺庙烧⑦掉，把和尚们都杀光。

① 发愁 (fāchóu) v. worry, be anxious
e.g., 他没了工作，很发愁。

② 将军 (jiāngjūn) n. general
e.g., 他从小就想当将军。

③ 造反 (zàofǎn) v. rebel
e.g., 这个将军造反了。

④ 抢劫 (qiǎngjié) v. rob
e.g., 这些造反的人到处抢劫。

⑤ 派 (pài) v. send, dispatch
e.g., 老师派我去拿东西。

⑥ 军队 (jūnduì) n. army, troops
e.g., 这是一支人民的军队。

⑦ 烧 (shāo) v. burn
e.g., 他把那些纸烧掉了。

① 叛军 (pànjūn) n. rebel forces
e.g., 这些叛军造反了，到处抢劫。

② 吓坏 (xiàhuài) v. be terrified
e.g., 这个孩子找不到自己的妈妈，吓坏了。

莺莺正在房间想着这几天发生的事，突然老夫人、长老都来敲门。开了门，老夫人哭着说："孩子，不好了，现在叛军①孙飞虎派兵围住了寺庙，要抢你去做妻子，怎么办啊？"听了母亲的话，莺莺也吓坏②了，不知道怎么办。母女两人只能抱在一起哭。

哭了一会儿，莺莺说："妈妈，把我送给叛军吧，要不不光我们全家人有危险，寺庙的人都活不了。"老夫人说："这怎么行？我只有你一个女儿，怎么能让你嫁①给叛军呢？"

莺莺想了想，说："妈妈，那还有一个办法。寺庙里有很多人，您和长老去告诉大家，要是有人能够打退叛军，就把我嫁给他。我想这样可能有人会想出办法。"

"这个办法还可以考虑一下，总比嫁给叛军好。"老夫人和长老赶紧来到大殿，对着大家大声说："如果有人可以打退叛军，老夫人就把自己的女儿莺莺

① 嫁 (jià) *v.*
marry (a husband)
e.g., 二十岁的时候，她嫁给了自己的男朋友。

① 抓 (zhuā) *v.* catch
e.g., 小偷想跑，但是很快被抓住了。

② 不慌不忙 (bùhuāng-bùmáng) unhurriedly
e.g., 大家都很紧张，他却不慌不忙。

嫁给他。"

听到可以和莺莺结婚，张生想也不想就站起来说："我有办法，我有办法！"老夫人很高兴，赶紧问："你有什么办法？"张生说："这里人多，请长老和老夫人到房间里商量。"

莺莺听说张生有办法打退叛军，心里又高兴又担心："希望张生真能成功。可是他只是个读书人，怎么打得过叛军呢，他不会被叛军抓①住吧？唉……"莺莺又伤心地哭了起来。

进了房间，老夫人、长老着急地问张生："张先生有什么好办法，赶紧说来听听。"张生不慌不忙②地说："我首先需要长老出去面对叛军……"长老一听就吓白了脸:"我就是一个和尚,怎么打退叛军,先生还是让别人去吧。"

张生一笑:"不是让您出去拼命①,是让您现在出去跟叛军说句话,您就说'崔小姐的父亲去世不久,她要做三天法事纪念②父亲。请你们退兵③三十里,

① 拼命 (pīnmìng)
v. risk one's life, do something with all one's might
e.g., 为了抓住那个人,他拼命往前跑。

② 纪念 (jìniàn) *v.* commemorate
e.g., 他写了一首诗,来纪念自己的父亲。

③ 退兵 (tuìbīng) *v.* retreat
e.g., 三天以后,将军终于决定退兵。

① 答应 (dāying) *v.* promise, agree
e.g., 答应我，不要爱上别人。

② 解围 (jiěwéi) *v.* lift a siege, get somebody out of a fix
e.g., 他遇到了很大的困难，多亏有人帮他解围。

③ 紧急 (jǐnjí) *adj.* urgent
e.g., 情况很紧急，他只能自己做决定。

三天之后，崔小姐就可以跟你们走。要不然的话，她就算死也不会答应①。我想这样叛军就会暂时退兵。"长老照着张生的话去跟叛军说，叛军听了后马上退兵，说三天以后再来。

长老和老夫人接着问张生："三天以后怎么办呢？张先生快告诉我们吧。"张生自信地说："我有一个同学，名叫杜确，人称'白马将军'，他的军队就在附近。我写一封信给他，他一定会带兵来解围②。"长老和老夫人一听都非常高兴，"情况紧急③，张先生赶紧写吧。"

张生写好信以后，长老选了最勇敢的一个和尚，

派他骑马把信给杜将军送去。过了两天,杜将军带着军队来到寺庙,把叛军打退了。大家都非常感谢张生,张生也非常高兴。"真的能和莺莺在一起了,这比考上状元①还让人高兴!不知道老夫人什么时候会安排我们的婚礼②,时间过得快点吧……"

① 状元 (zhuàngyuan) n. Champion Graduate, title conferred to the one who placed first in the highest imperial civil examination
e.g., 这次考试他考了第一名,得了状元。

② 婚礼 (hūnlǐ) n. wedding ceremony
e.g., 他们结婚的那天办了一个盛大的婚礼。

① 整整齐齐 (zhěngzhěngqíqí) adv. neatly
e.g., 今天他毕业，所以他穿得整整齐齐。

② 盼 (pàn) v. long for, expect
e.g., 他一直盼着自己的妻子回来。

四、老夫人请客，夫妻变兄妹

这一天，张生穿得整整齐齐①，在房间走来走去。"老夫人怎么还不来请我，什么时候让我和莺莺结婚呢？"正想着，红娘来了。互相问好以后，张生问："姑娘找我有什么事？"红娘笑着说："张先生退了叛军，老夫人特意派我来请您去我们那里吃晚饭。请问张先生有时间吗？"

张生一听，立刻回答："有时间，有时间！马上就可以去。"

"他不知道已经盼②了多长时间呢？"红娘心想。"那就请先生一定去，我先回去了。"

张生还是有点不放心，接着问："这次请客，老夫人要说什么呢？"

"当然是你心里想的事，就是你和莺莺姐姐的婚事啦！"红娘笑着说。

"可是我只是个穷书生，没钱也没地位，老夫人真的会把莺莺嫁给我吗？"张生担心地问。

"放心吧，你救了我们家，我们夫人和姐姐都是说话算话的人，一定会答应你们的婚事的。"红娘回答。

晚上，张生来到老夫人这里做客。老夫人很热情地接待张生，说："这次打退叛军，救了我们崔家，全靠张先生。来，我给张

① 亲自 (qīnzi) adv.
in person
e.g., 国王亲自迎接将军回来。

② 果然 (guǒrán) adv.
as expected, really
e.g., 他果然来了。

③ 算数 (suànshù) v.
count, hold
e.g., 他说话不算数，你不要相信他。

先生倒酒。"张生赶紧说："不敢，不敢，怎么能让老夫人亲自①倒酒呢？"老夫人不听，给张生倒了酒，回头对红娘说："去，叫小姐出来，给张先生行礼。"张生心里非常激动，"老夫人果然②说话算数③，这是要我和莺莺成婚吧。"

红娘来到莺莺房间，说："姐姐，老夫人让你去见一位先生。"

莺莺想了想，说："我有点不舒服，就不去了。"

红娘笑着说："你不问问是谁吗？"

"是谁？"莺莺装作①不关心的样子。

"是张生，姐姐不去就算了。"红娘假装要走。

听到张生来了，莺莺马上站了起来。"你等一下，我感觉好多了，这就去。"

莺莺一边走一边想："多亏了张生，救了我们全家。希望我母亲说话算数，能让我和张生在一起……"

"姐姐，你今天可真漂亮。张生真是有福气②

① 装作 (zhuāngzuò) *v.* pretend
e.g., 他装作很生气的样子，其实他没有生气。

② 福气 (fúqi) *n.* luck, blessing
e.g., 你真有福气，娶了这么漂亮的妻子。

① 相思病
(xiāngsībìng) n.
lovesickness
e.g., 他爱上了一个女孩儿，得了相思病。

② 自言自语
(zìyán-zìyǔ)
talk to oneself
e.g., 没有人和他聊天，他常常自言自语。

③ 婚宴 (hūnyàn) n.
wedding banquet
e.g., 婚宴是婚礼的时候举办的宴会。

啊！"红娘在莺莺的耳边说。

"不该说的别乱说！"莺莺假装生气地说。

到了会客厅，张生和莺莺的眼光碰在一起，又马上分开了。

红娘看看莺莺，又看看张生，小声说："哎，往常两个人都得了相思病①，天天伤心，今天终于开心了。"

莺莺自言自语②地说："以后可以不用相思，一直在一起了。"

红娘又有点担心地小声问："姐姐，结婚这么大的事，为什么老夫人不安排婚宴③，只是简单请客呢？"

莺莺想了一下，说：

"我妈比较爱钱,可能安排婚宴要花不少钱,张生又没有钱,就这样安排了。"

老夫人把莺莺拉到张生面前,张生满心欢喜①也非常激动,莺莺则害羞地把头扭②到一边去。大家都等着老夫人宣布③两个人结婚,却听老夫人说:"莺莺,给你的哥哥行礼。"

"哥哥?怎么变成哥哥了?!难道是我母亲改主意了?"莺莺心里一惊,不知道怎么办才好。

"叫我哥哥?难道这老太太说话不算数了?"张生心里也凉④了,"一定是嫌我没钱没地位。"

"哎呀,老夫人改主意了!唉,相思病治⑤不好

① 欢喜 (huānxǐ) *adj.*
joyful, happy
e.g., 听到这个消息,他心里非常欢喜。

② 扭 (niǔ) *v.*
turn around
e.g., 看到那个男孩,她扭头走了。

③ 宣布 (xuānbù) *v.*
announce, declare
e.g., 政府宣布了新的政策。

④ 凉 (liáng) *adj.* cold
e.g., 听到这个消息,他心里就凉了。

⑤ 治 (zhì) *v.*
cure, treat
e.g., 这种病很难治。

① 默默 (mòmò) *adj.* quiet, silent
e.g., 他默默地听着，一句话也不说。

② 含 (hán) *v.* bear, hold in the mouth
e.g., 他的嘴里含着水，说话不清楚。

了。"红娘叹了口气。

三个人都在发愣，老夫人说："莺莺，快给你哥哥倒酒。"莺莺到张生面前，默默①地倒了一杯酒。

老夫人笑着说："以后你们俩就是兄妹了，莺莺，你回房间去吧。"莺莺眼里含②着泪水，转身回房间去了。

张生把酒一口喝完，说："老夫人，我想问问您，前几天你说谁能把叛军打退，就把莺莺嫁给谁，今天为什么反悔①呢？"老夫人坐下来，慢慢地说："张先生，你确实救了我们一家。不过，我丈夫活着的时候，已经约②好把莺莺嫁给我的侄子③郑恒了。所以我让你们结为兄妹，我给你一笔钱，你可以去找更好的女孩……"

"老夫人，我救莺莺不是为了钱。我喝醉④了，先告辞⑤了。"张生脑子里一片空白。老夫人说："那我就不留先生了，红娘，扶⑥张先生回去。"

五、莺莺夜听琴

① 反悔 (fǎnhuǐ) v. go back on one's word, pull back
e.g., 本来他答应和她结婚，没想到后来他又反悔了。

② 约 (yuē) v. make an appointment
e.g., 他约了一个好朋友一起吃饭。

③ 侄子 (zhízi) n. nephew (the son of one's brother)
e.g., 自己弟弟或哥哥的儿子叫作侄子。

④ 喝醉 (hēzuì) get drunk
e.g., 他喝了很多酒，喝醉了。

⑤ 告辞 (gàocí) v. bid farewell
e.g., 要离开的时候可以说"我要告辞了"。

⑥ 扶 (fú) v. support (with hands)
e.g., 他的腿受伤了，走路需要别人扶。

① 委屈 (wěiqu) *n.* grievance
e.g., 这些年他受了很多委屈。

② 跪 (guì) *v.* kneel
e.g., 结婚的时候, 孩子要给自己的父母跪下。

张生由红娘扶着,往自己的房间走去。红娘说:"张生,你就不能少喝点吗,醉成这样。"

张生一肚子委屈①,突然跪②下来大声说:"红娘,你不知道我的心事吗?为了莺莺,我吃不下睡不着。本来以为这次终于可以得到莺莺了,你们老夫人又

说话不算话！我也活不下去了，不如死在你面前吧，麻烦你把我的心意告诉莺莺，我这就去上吊①。"

红娘又好气又好笑，"你这个傻瓜，遇到这么点困难就要死吗？你别着急，我给你想想办法。"

"有什么办法？快说呀！"张生着急地看着红娘。

红娘想了一会儿，说："想出来了！我家小姐最喜欢听琴，我记得你会弹琴②。今天我和小姐去花园烧香，我一咳嗽，你就开始弹。看看听到琴声小姐会怎么说。"

"嗯，只能这样试试了。"张生回到房间，抱着自己的琴睡着了。

① 上吊 (shàngdiào)
v. hang oneself
e.g., 那个人上吊自杀了。

② 弹琴 (tán qín) play instrument
e.g., 他从小就学习弹琴。

① 倾诉 (qīngsù)
v. pour out (one's heart, troubles, worries, etc.)
e.g., 他特别难过，需要找人倾诉。

② 凤求凰 (Fèng Qiú Huáng) *A Male Phoenix Seeks His Mate* is a *guqin* piece written during the Han Dynasty (206 BC-AD 220). It tells the story of two lovers who eloped. Phoenix is the legendary bird, and 凤 refers to the male phoenix while 凰 refers to the female one.

月亮出来了，又大又亮。张生在房间里摸着自己的琴，自言自语地说："琴啊，你跟着我这么多年，今天晚上就看你的了，让我弹出优美的琴声飘到莺莺的耳朵里，让她能听到我的心声。"正想着，突然听到一声咳嗽。

"来了！"张生立刻打起精神，弹起琴来。

莺莺和红娘正在烧香，听到琴声，莺莺奇怪地说："哪来的琴声呢？这么动听，像是在倾诉①心里的感情……"

红娘说："姐姐你在这里听琴，我去看看老夫人。"

这时张生开始弹《凤求凰》②，他一边弹，一边唱："有位美人，见过难忘。

一天不见，想得发狂。凤飞天上，四处找凰……[3]"

莺莺也听出了这个曲子①。"这一定是张生，他是在用琴声表达②他的心声啊。"莺莺想到她和张生的第一次见面，想到张生打退叛军的勇敢，想到母亲反悔的事情，她的眼泪流了下来。

① 曲子 (qǔzi) n. tune
e.g., 这首曲子特别好听。

② 表达 (biǎodá) v. express, convey
e.g., 他很想表达自己的感谢，但是不知道怎么说。

① 怨 (yuàn) *v.* blame
e.g., 心情不好的时候，他总是怨别人。

莺莺对着琴声的方向说：“张生，你的心事我知道。”

琴声停下来，张生说：“莺莺，你真的知道吗？不是骗我吗？”

莺莺哭着说："我当然知道。你别怨①我，反悔是我母亲的主意，我也没有办法……"

正说着，红娘跑过来说："姐姐，老夫人在找你，咱们快回去吧。"莺莺一边走一边回头，琴声又响了起来。

六、红娘传情书

张生病了,躺在床上一点精神都没有。他正躺着,突然有人敲门。

"是谁?"张生有气无力地问。

"我是专治相思病的大夫!"接着是一阵笑声,红娘走了进来。

一看是红娘,张生有了一些精神,问:"你家小姐这几天怎么样?"

"我家小姐啊,"红娘笑着说,"跟你差不多,都得了相思病,早上还没吃饭已经叫了'张生'好几百遍了。"

听到这些,张生坐了起来:"既然小姐也对我有意,我这里有一封信,里

① 翻脸 (fānliǎn) v. fall out with sb. e.g., 为了一件小事,他和自己的朋友翻脸了。

② 撕 (sī) v. tear e.g., 生气的时候,他把那本书撕了。

面是我写给莺莺的诗,你可不可以帮我拿给她?"

"这样好吗?我了解我们小姐,直接给她情诗她会翻脸①的,一定会把信撕②了的。"红娘有点为难。

张生急着说:"你一定要帮我的忙,等有了钱,我买好多礼物送给你。"

红娘一下子就生气了,"我帮你的忙是为了钱吗?

我是看你可怜，也觉得你和我家小姐挺合适的，我才这样帮你们。"

张生赶紧说："那姐姐你就可怜可怜我吧，要不我都活不下去了……"

红娘说："好吧，你放心，我一定拿给她。"

红娘拿着张生的信，想："怎么给小姐呢？如果直接给她，她一定会发火的。不如把信放在镜子上，她照镜子的时候就会看见。"

莺莺来照镜子，看见有一封信就打开来看，只见信上有一首诗："想念多又多，弹琴表心情。春天多美好，让我心也动。爱情来敲门，怎能不放行？

① 负 (fù) *v.* fail to live up to, disappoint
e.g., 你不要负了她的一片深情。

② 皱眉 (zhòuméi) *v.* frown
e.g., 他有点生气，皱起了眉。

莫负①月光明，快来看花影。[4]"莺莺一看就知道写的是自己和张生的事情，也猜到信是张生写的。

红娘在一边小心地看着莺莺的反应，只见莺莺开始时羞红了脸，然后又皱起了眉②，突然大叫一声："红娘，过来！"

"不好，小姐果然要发火。"红娘赶紧走过去，"怎么了姐姐？"

莺莺一脸愤怒①地说："怎么了？我问你，这封信是哪里来的？我是相国的女儿，怎么能写这样的诗给我，我要告诉老夫人，看她怎么教训②你！"

红娘知道莺莺是故意装出生气的样子，就无所谓③地说："好吧，我自己把信拿去给老夫人看，就说是张生写的……"

"哎，红娘，别，别，我逗④你玩呢。"莺莺换了一副笑脸，"快跟我说说，张生最近怎么样？"

红娘说："张生现在吃不下饭，睡不着觉，瘦的不得了，从早到晚对着咱们这边流眼泪……"

"啊，这么严重，我让

① 愤怒 (fènnù) *adj.* indignant
e.g., 听到别人这样说他，他愤怒地站了起来。

② 教训 (jiàoxùn) *v.* admonish, lecture somebody
e.g., 孩子犯了错误，爸爸认真教训了他一顿。

③ 无所谓 (wúsuǒwèi) be indifferent
e.g., 去或是不去，他都无所谓。

④ 逗 (dòu) *v.* tease, trick
e.g., 他正在逗一个小孩子玩儿。

人请个医生给他看看吧。"莺莺有点担心,然后又说,"红娘,我和张生没有什么事,只是老夫人让我们像兄妹一样相处,所以我得关心他一下。"

红娘笑了起来,"你骗谁呀,要真是兄妹,张生哪能病成这样。"

莺莺赶紧说:"好红娘,这件事不要告诉我母亲啊,她知道了可不得了。这样吧,我给张生写一封回信。你告诉他,我只把他当作哥哥看,以后不要再给我写这样的诗了,要不然我就告诉老夫人去。"说完莺莺拿来纸和笔,写了一封回信。

七、张生猜谜语①

红娘拿着莺莺的信来找张生。

"红娘来啦,怎么样了?小姐怎么说?"张生着急地问。

红娘无奈②地说:"张生,你先有点心理准备。小姐看了信很生气,说她只把你当哥哥,以后再不要给她写信。我也没有办法。"

"啊?怎么会这样呢?到底是怎么回事,红娘,你得帮帮我啊!"张生又跪在红娘面前,拉着红娘的衣服哭了起来。

红娘说:"唉,真拿你没有办法。这是小姐给你的回信,你自己看吧。"

---

① 谜语 (míyǔ) n. riddle
e.g., 他出了一个谜语,但是没有人猜出来。

② 无奈 (wúnài) v. resign oneself to
e.g., 面对这种情况,他也很无奈。

张生赶紧打开信，发现莺莺也写了一首诗："等月西厢下，风吹门半开。墙上花影动，疑是美人来。"[5]张生看了又看，想了又想，突然说："红娘，我要大大地感谢你啊！小姐那么骂我是假的，她的诗其实是让我今天晚上和她去约会呢！"

"你怎么看出来的？"红娘奇怪地问。

张生有点得意，说："我是猜谜语的专家。你看——第一句的意思是约会时间是月亮出来的时候；第二句的意思是她开门等我；第三、四句的意思是让我跳墙过去，和她见面。哎呀，太好了！我这就去跳墙。"

红娘说:"现在才中午啊。"

"什么时候天黑呀?"张生盼着太阳下山,月亮出来。

红娘回到房间,心想:"小姐瞒①着我写诗约张生,我也不说破,看她今天怎么做。"于是她对莺莺说:"姐姐,月亮出来了,咱们去花园烧香吧。"莺莺看看月亮,说:"今天月亮好圆,夜色好美。"红娘心想:"我看你和张生差不多,都盼着天黑呢。"

两人来到花园,莺莺开始烧香。红娘偷偷来到墙角,把角门打开。"按照那个谜语,张生应该从

① 瞒 (mán) v. conceal something
e.g., 他瞒着父母结了婚。

① 狂喜 (kuángxǐ) *adj.* wild with joy
e.g., 听到这个好消息，他一阵狂喜。

这儿进来，不知道他来了没有。"

张生其实早早就等在墙边，等着墙那边莺莺来了，就翻墙过去。突然墙边的角门开了。"莺莺给我开门了！她真的对我有意思！"张生一阵狂喜①。张

生从门过去来到墙这边,看到一个美丽的人影。"莺莺!"张生一下子把那美人抱住了。

"放开!你这个禽兽①,我是红娘!"那美人叫了一声。

张生一看果然是红娘,赶紧道歉:"对不起!对不起!我抱得太快了,没看清。"

红娘整理②了一下衣服,小声说:"真讨厌!小姐在湖边③,快去吧。"

张生走到湖边,见莺莺果然在那里烧香。他慢慢走过去,一下子抱住了莺莺。莺莺一惊:"是谁?"

"是我呀,张生。"

莺莺把张生推开,生

① 禽兽 (qínshòu) n. beast, dirty swine
e.g., 女人经常骂男人"禽兽"。

② 整理 (zhěnglǐ) v. tidy
e.g., 他正在整理房间。

③ 湖边 (hú biān) n. lakeside
e.g., 湖边有好多树。

① 告 (gào) v.
tell, complain, report
e.g., 他受了委屈，就告到了老师那里。

气地说："张生，你把我当成什么人了！我在这里烧香，你来做什么？你是读书人，不知道男女授受不亲吗？"接着莺莺转身朝红娘喊："红娘，有贼，咱们快走。"

红娘一看莺莺翻了脸，赶紧过来，假装生气地骂张生："张生，没想到你是这样的人！快过来给小姐跪下道歉，不然我们告①到老夫人那里，看你怎么办。"

看着两个翻脸的女人，张生满脸通红，脑子里一片空白，一句话也说不出来，只好跪下给莺莺道歉。

莺莺说："张生，我母

亲让我把你当哥哥一样,这次就算了,以后再这样,我一定告诉我母亲。红娘,咱们回去!"

红娘把张生拉起来,小声说:"还说自己是猜谜的专家①,这次猜错了吧。"

张生一脸苦笑:"女人的谜太难猜,不想猜了。"

① 专家 (zhuānjiā) n. expert
e.g., 他是一个语言专家。

① 药方 (yàofāng) *n.* prescription
e.g., 医生给他开了一个药方。

八、莺莺张生月夜相会

莺莺在房间里照镜子，想着心事。

"姐姐，今天听老夫人说，张生这次真的病了，请了好多医生来呢。"红娘对莺莺说。

"真的吗，那么严重？红娘你去看看他吧。"莺莺担心地说。

红娘"哼"了一声："还不是你把人家骂一顿才成了这样，我看这次他是受了很大的打击。"

莺莺站了起来："这样，红娘，我给他写一个药方①，你给他送去，他一定会好。"

红娘说："姐姐，你又不是医生，怎么会开药方。

再说,你们闹①成这样,我也不想给你们当邮差②了。"

"好红娘,这次一定要帮我,要不张生一病不起怎么办。你放心,我这药方肯定有效果。"莺莺求着红娘。

"好吧,再帮你们最后一次,把药方给我吧。"红娘无奈地说。

张生在床上躺着,想起莺莺的话,觉得自己一点希望都没有了。"女人怎么总是这样变来变去呢,真是猜不透③"。正想着,红娘来了。

"张先生好点了吗?"红娘问。

张生一脸苦笑:"好不了了。我真是被你们两个

① 闹 (nào) v.
make a scene
e.g., 他看到哥哥的苹果大,不高兴闹了起来。

② 邮差 (yóuchāi) n.
mailman
e.g., 邮差专门给人送信。

③ 透 (tòu) adj.
clear, through
e.g., 女人的想法有时候猜不透。

女人害死了。"

红娘叹了一口气:"天下得相思病的那么多,没见过你这样要死要活的。我这里有小姐给你的药方,看看能不能治你的病。"

"药方?"张生一下子坐起来,接过红娘手里的信,信上还是写着一首诗:"莫把闲事放心怀,浪费才华真不该。当时只为救我

命，今日害你惹祸灾。一心想谢大恩情，写下新诗来表白。不用再做相思梦。今晚请你等我来。[6]"

"太好了！"张生一拍手站了起来，"今天晚上莺莺会来找我的！"

"真的吗？你这个猜谜专家又猜对谜语了？"红娘开张生的玩笑。

"这次肯定猜对，放心吧！"张生兴奋地说，"回去告诉小姐，我完全好了，现在就收拾收拾房间。"

月亮出来了，莺莺对红娘说："红娘，天晚了，咱们睡吧。"

红娘笑着说："睡了？那个傻瓜怎么办，你又要骗人家？"

① 撇嘴 (piězuǐ) v.
purse one's lips
e.g., 她撇了撇嘴，哭了。

② 折磨 (zhémó) v.
torture
e.g., 为了和崔莺莺在一起，张生受了很多折磨。

"哪个傻瓜？"莺莺的脸红了。

"别装了。"红娘撇撇嘴①，"我去看看老夫人睡了没有，等她睡了就去找你的心上人。"

莺莺红着脸不说话。

过了一会儿，红娘回来了，说："姐姐，咱们走吧，老夫人睡了。"莺莺低着头，和红娘小心地往张生的房间走去。

张生在房间里等得心里像着了火。"今晚莺莺会来吗？要是来了，我就是世界上最幸福的人了；要是不来，我就是世界上最痛苦的人。唉，爱情真是折磨②人啊！"这时，他突然看到窗户上有人影。"莺莺来啦！"

张生赶紧出去迎接。

"张生,跪下感谢我。"红娘在那里开玩笑,"我把小姐给你带来了。"

张生赶紧跪下,"感谢红娘姐姐成全!"莺莺把张生拉起来。张生握着莺莺的手,看着她美丽的脸,说:"我这是在做梦吗?"莺莺羞红了脸,和张生进了房间,两个有情人①终于在一起了。

① **有情人** (yǒuqíngrén)
n. lover
e.g., 张生和崔莺莺是一对有情人。

① 观察 (guānchá) v. observe, watch
e.g., 小孩常常观察身边的动物。

② 嘴硬 (zuǐyìng) adj. stubborn and reluctant to admit mistakes or defeats
e.g., 他一直很嘴硬，从来不承认自己的错误。

九、老夫人同意婚事，张生进京考试

老夫人这几天一直在观察①莺莺，觉得莺莺有些奇怪，好像总是在想事情，有时候还忍不住笑一声。身边有人告诉老夫人，莺莺和红娘每晚去花园烧香，总是很晚回来。"难道她和张生有什么事？"老夫人有些担心，"去把红娘找来，我要问她事情。"

红娘来到老夫人这里，看到老夫人满脸愤怒。"红娘，跪下！你不知道自己犯的错吗？"

"不知道，我没犯错！"红娘抬起头，看着老夫人。

"还嘴硬②！说，你每天晚上带着小姐去哪儿了，是不是去找张生了？你要是说实话还好，要是不说实话，我就打死你！"说着，老夫人让手下人打红娘。

红娘被打了几下，举手说："别打了，老夫人，我有话说。"

"你说吧。"老夫人让手下人停手。红娘不紧不慢地说："老夫人，小姐确实是和张生在一起了，但是这件事是您的不对。"

① 世世代代
(shìshìdàidài)
generations
e.g., 他们家世世代代都是读书人。

② 贵族 (guìzú) *n.*
nobility
e.g., 他是贵族出身。

"我的不对？"老夫人更生气了。

"是啊，"红娘接着说，"您本来就答应了张生，打退叛军就把小姐嫁给他。结果您说话不算数，让他们俩当兄妹，这是您的第一个错误。打退叛军以后，就应该让张生和小姐离得远一点，结果我们还住在这里，男有情，女有意，早晚会出事，这是您的第二个错误。现在事情已经这样了，您最好的办法就是同意他们俩的事，把小姐正式嫁给张生。"

"我们家世世代代①都是贵族②，莺莺怎么能嫁给那个穷小子呢？"老夫人摇摇头。

"老夫人，别看张生现在是个穷书生，但他人聪明，学习好，以后一定能中状元，当大官，小姐嫁给他也未必是坏事。再说，他们俩已经在一起了，小姐只喜欢张生，怕是不会再嫁给别人了。"红娘接着劝老夫人。

　　老夫人觉得红娘说得有道理，只能叹口气，说："唉，这个不听话的孩子啊，做出这样的事。我也只能同意把我这女儿嫁给那个穷书生了。"

　　老夫人叫红娘把莺莺和张生叫来，同意了他们的婚事，但提了一个要求，就是张生必须马上离开，去京城参加考试，取得功

① 功名 (gōngmíng) *n.* scholarly honor and official rank e.g., 没有取得功名，他是不会回家的。

② 订婚 (dìnghūn) *v.* be engaged to e.g., 他们交往半年后订婚了。

名①后才能回来和莺莺结婚。张生不愿意和莺莺分开，但为了能和莺莺结婚，只能答应了。

第二天，莺莺、红娘、老夫人、长老等人都来给张生送别。

老夫人说："张生，我把我的女儿嫁给了你，你这次考试一定要中个状元回来才对得起她。"

张生说："母亲，您放心，这次我一定中个状元回来。"

红娘给莺莺倒上一杯酒，莺莺举起酒杯，还没说话，已经是泪流满面，"你我刚刚订婚②就要分别。你去京城，不知道什么时候才能回来。张生，不管这次能不能考中状元,考完之后就快回来。"

张生也流下了眼泪,"你放心,考完我马上就回来,你在家等我的好消息。"哭完之后,张生骑上马,一步几回头地向前走了。张生走出去很远,似乎还可以看到莺莺的影子。

这时候一阵秋风吹过,黄叶满天,一行大雁① 由北向南飞过。

① **大雁** (dàyàn) *n.* wild goose
e.g., 大雁是一种候鸟,冬天会飞到南方。

① 眷属 (juànshǔ) n. husband and wife
e.g., 有情人终成眷属，崔莺莺和张生终于在一起了。

② 思念 (sīniàn) v. miss
e.g., 他常常思念自己的父母。

十、有情人终成眷属①

张生一走就是半年，莺莺每天都在思念②张生。"考试应该结束了，张生考得怎样？他怎么还不回来呢？会不会爱上别的女人？"

正想着，红娘跑过来说："姐姐，郑恒来了。就是老夫人的侄子，之前和你订婚的那个。"

"郑恒？他怎么来了？"莺莺心里有点担心，"你去听听他跟我母亲说什么。"

红娘来到老夫人房间，看到郑恒正在哭，问老夫人为什么不把莺莺嫁给他。老夫人有点不好意思地把事情经过告诉了郑恒。

郑恒擦擦眼泪，问："姑姑①，您是说莺莺跟张生订婚了？这个张生去京城考试了？"

老夫人说："是啊，已经去了半年了，不知道他考得怎么样。"

郑恒说："我刚从京城来，那个张生中了状元，然后被卫尚书看中了，卫尚书把女儿嫁给他了。全城的人都知道。"

"真的吗？"老夫人气坏了，"我早说这个家伙②不是好人，最后还是把我女儿抛弃③了。侄儿，我还是把莺莺嫁给你。"

"谢谢姑姑！我一定好好对待莺莺。"郑恒笑了起来。

① 姑姑 (gūgu) aunt (father's sister)
e.g., 孩子管爸爸的姐妹叫姑姑。

② 家伙 (jiāhuo) *n.* fellow, guy
e.g., 他是一个坏家伙。

③ 抛弃 (pāoqì) *v.* abandon, desert
e.g., 不要抛弃你的狗。

① 娶 (qǔ) *v.*
marry (a wife)
e.g., 他还没娶老婆。

红娘赶紧跑回莺莺的房间告诉莺莺:"姐姐不好了! 老夫人又要把你嫁给郑恒了!"

"怎么会? 母亲不是答应了张生吗?"莺莺着急地问。

"你不知道,那个郑恒说,张生中了状元,然后又娶①了卫尚书的女儿,留在京城不要咱们了！"红娘生气地解释。

"真的是这样吗？我们的感情他都忘了吗？"莺莺哭了起来。

不管莺莺愿不愿意，老夫人还是决定把莺莺嫁给郑恒。这一天，老夫人命令手下人准备宴席①，给郑恒和莺莺办婚礼。

正准备着，突然门外有人喊："河中府尹②张生大人③到！"只见张生高高兴兴地走进寺庙，看见老夫人就跪下，说："母亲大人，我这次去京城赶考中了状元，当了河中府尹，现在来接您和莺莺！"

老夫人生气地说："府尹大人快起来吧，听说您

① 宴席 (yànxí) *n.* banquet
e.g., 今天是我妈妈的生日，我们家大摆筵席。

② 府尹 (fǔyǐn) *n.* prefecture governor
e.g., 府尹相当于现在的市长。

③ 大人 (dàren) *n.* lord
e.g., 大人，我冤枉啊！

已经娶了卫尚书的女儿了，这不，我正要把女儿嫁给郑恒呢。"

"啊？卫尚书的女儿？谁说的呀？"看到红娘在旁边，张生赶紧问红娘，"红娘，这是怎么回事呀？"

"你还有脸问我？"红娘生气地说，"快跟我说

说，你的新夫人怎样啊，比我姐姐漂亮吗？"

"哎呀，哪有这样的事呀，到底是谁说的？"张生着急地问。

"是老夫人的侄子郑恒。你真的没有娶别人吗？"红娘问。

"要是我娶了别人，就让我不得好死！红娘你相信我吗？"张生认真地说。

"嗯，我相信你。这样，我和你一起去找姐姐，然后当面问问郑恒，看他是不是在撒谎①。"红娘看着张生说。

房间里莺莺正在哭。张生走到莺莺面前，说："莺莺，那个郑恒是在撒谎，我根本没有娶什么卫

① 撒谎 (sāhuǎng) v. lie
e.g., 他经常撒谎，大家都不相信他。

尚书的女儿。"红娘也在旁边说:"对,我也相信张生,咱们再去问问郑恒,看他说的是不是真的。"

三人正说着,张生的老朋友白马将军杜确来了。杜将军说:"张生,听说你中了状元,当了河中府尹,我特意来给你祝贺。"张生一看是杜确,非常高兴:"杜将军,你来得正好,你知道京城的情况,可以证明我没有和什么卫尚书的女儿结婚,对不对?"

"卫尚书的女儿?哪有这样的事,我可以证明,张生一考完就回来了,一心想着自己的未婚妻莺莺。"杜确肯定地说。

红娘说:"那就是那

个郑恒说谎了,这个大坏蛋①,他跑到哪里去了!"

外面有仆人来报告②说:"那个郑恒知道自己撒谎被发现,已经逃走了。"

杜将军非常生气,想派兵把他抓回来。老夫人说:"算了,他毕竟③是我的侄子,看在我的面子④上,

① 坏蛋 (huàidàn) n.
scoundrel, rascal
e.g., 你这个坏蛋,做什么对不起我的事了?

② 报告 (bàogào) v.
report
e.g., 你应该把事情的经过向领导报告。

③ 毕竟 (bìjìng) adv.
after all
e.g., 她毕竟是你的女儿。

④ 面子 (miànzi) n.
face, reputation
e.g., 你这样让我很没面子。

① **说情** (shuōqíng) *v.* plead for mercy for sb. e.g., 你们不用帮他说情，他是什么人我心里清楚。

放了他吧。"张生和莺莺也帮着说情①，最后杜将军就放走了郑恒。

张生和崔莺莺终于可以幸福地在一起了，再也没有人可以把他们分开。

[1] original poem：月色溶溶夜，花阴寂寂春；如何临皓魄，不见月中人？

[2] original poem：兰闺久寂寞，无事度芳春；料得行吟者，应怜长叹人。

[3] original lyrics：有美人兮，见之不忘。一日不见兮，思之如狂。凤飞翱翱兮，四海求凰。

[4] original poem：相思恨转添，谩把瑶琴弄。乐事又逢春，芳心尔亦动。此情不可违，芳誉何须奉？莫负月华明，且怜花影重。

[5] original poem：待月西厢下，迎风户半开。隔墙花影动，疑是玉人来。

[6] original poem：休将闲事苦萦怀，取次摧残天赋才。不意当时完妾命，岂防今日作君灾？仰图厚德难从礼，谨奉新诗可当谋。寄语高唐休咏赋，今宵端的雨云来。

English Version

Romance of the West Chamber

1. Zhang Sheng Meets Cui Yingying

Zhang Sheng, a scholar in the Tang Dynasty, was on his way to Chang'an, the capital, for the imperial civil examination. A place called Hezhong Prefecture was on his route. The place had a renowned monastery called Pujiu Monastery (Universal Salvation Monastery). Zhang decided to take this opportunity to pay it a visit.

When Zhang was looking around the monastery, he walked into a small garden where a beautiful young lady was plucking a flower. She was about 18 or 19 years old with breathtaking beauty. Zhang was amazed and thought, "Is it possible that such a beauty is an earthly human being? Is she a fairy from heaven?" Then a maid-like young girl also came to the garden. She was pretty as well; however, the two did not linger much longer and soon left the garden.

Zhang wasted no time in finding a young monk and asked, "There are fairies in your garden, right?" The monk answered surprisingly, "What fairies?" Zhang said, "The lady who was plucking flowers in the garden. Isn't she a fairy?" The monk said with a smile, "She isn't a fairy. Her name is Cui Yingying. She is the daughter of Mr. Cui, the late Counselor-in-Chief. Her father passed away, so she and her mother are having his coffin carried to their hometown. They are staying here because they have some matter to attend to." Zhang added, "Then, who is the other girl?" The monk replied, "Oh, it must be Hongniang, Miss Cui's maid."

At night, Zhang couldn't sleep, as he couldn't shake the image of the young lady from his mind. "Cui Yingying," he repeated her name over and over. He thought, "It never occurred to me that I could encounter such a beauty here. How wonderful it would be if we could be together! I must get to know her. Would her maid be of any assistance? For her sake, I must stay in the monastery, no matter the cost!" With that resolution, Zhang gradually fell asleep.

Zhang went to visit the elder of the monastery the next day and asked to lodge there after paying the elder one tael of silver. The elder said, "We have many rooms available. You can stay here." During their conversation, a girl dropped by and asked, "Elder, Madam Cui inquired when you could deliver the religious service for the late Counselor-in-Chief?" Zhang raised his head and found it was Hongniang, the maid. The elder replied, "The fifteenth of this month could work."

Shortly after Hongniang left the elder's room, Zhang ran up to address her, "Good day, young lady." Hongniang replied politely, "Good day, sir. What can I do for you?" Zhang said, "Are you Miss Cui's maid?" She said, "Yes, I am. Who are you, sir?" Zhang said excitedly, "Oh…, I'm Zhang Sheng. I turned 23 years old this year. My birthday is on the seventeenth day of the first lunar month. I haven't been married yet …" "Who asked whether you are married or not!" Hongniang was angry, but was amused at the same time. Zhang found himself in an awkward situation, and he quickly explained, "I meant to ask if Miss Cui Yingying goes out often?" Hongniang was yet more irritated.

She said, "Your looks say you're an educated person. How could you be so rude? Don't you know that men and women should keep a proper distance from each other? How could you inquire about an unmarried lady? In the future, be aware of propriety and don't ask improper questions!" With that, she left without looking back. Seeing that she was walking away in anger, Zhang was filled with regret and said to himself, "This maid isn't very pleasant. How can I get in touch with Yingying? I need to think this through."

2. Writing Poems and Stealing Glances

Hongniang returned and told Madam Cui the arrangements for the service. She then went to the west chamber, where Yingying was staying. She said to Yingying, "Sister, let me tell you an interesting story. Today, I met a very interesting scholar in the monastery." Then she told Yingying about their conversation. Yingying also found it amusing and said, "Don't ever tell my mother about that. It's evening now, let's go to the garden to burn some incense."

The moonlight, like flowing water, shone upon the garden. Yingying lit some incense and prayed, "The first stick of incense is for my father to enter the realm of heaven; the second is for the good health and peace of my mother; the third …" Yingying paused. Hongniang hurried to add, "This one is for Sister Yingying to find a good husband." Yingying sighed and said nothing.

At that very moment, a man's voice was heard from the other side of the wall. The man chanted a poem, "The moonlight is like the flowing water, shining upon the quiet flowers. The moon seems near, but why can't one see the beauty living in the moon?" Hongniang quickly said, "Listen, it sounds like that unmarried, 23-year-old fool."

It turned out that the young monk told Zhang that Yingying burned incense in the garden every day. So he hid and waited in a corner of the garden. Hearing Yingying's prayer, he thought, "Yingying also longs for love. Perhaps she has feelings for me. Let me work out a poem and read it to her." So he composed a poem and read it aloud.

Yingying thought Zhang's poem was good. "Good lines!" She said, "I will write one in reply." She worked out a poem and read, "Alone I stay in the room, lonesome and bored. The one who chanted the poem, you should know my heart." Zhang was surprised to hear it, and thought, "Yingying responded to my poem so fast and so well. She is a combination of beauty and talent! I must go and meet her now!"

Zhang emerged from the corner. He walked up to Yingying with a big smile. Yingying was not surprised by his arrival and was about to speak. But Hongniang cut in, "Miss Cui, there comes a stranger. Let's leave immediately. Otherwise, Madam Cui will be angry." Yingying did not reply. She turned her back and went towards her room with Hongniang. Zhang's heart sank. He thought, "Well, why has the maid said that? She is so unhelpful." He was about to go back to his room in disappointment when he heard a rustling sound. "Has Yingying come back for me?" Zhang turned his back only to find a bird brushing by the flowers and flying into the sky. "Why am I so unlucky! How will I sleep tonight?"

Zhang had learned that Yingying's mother would have the religious service for the late Mr. Cui, so he hurried to the elder and offered to help during the service. The elder gave his consent.

On the day of the service, Zhang arrived early at the hall of the monastery. He saw a busy scene as the monks were chanting scriptures. He looked around for Yingying and found Madam Cui seated at the front with Yingying and Hongniang. Yingying was mourning her father. Zhang looked at Yingying stealthily while he helped in the service. With tears running down her face, Yingying looked like a flower with drops of rain on its petals, so beautiful. Zhang was so absorbed by her beauty, the elder had to distract him, "Zhang Sheng, the candle over there went out. Go and light it." Zhang was too embarrassed to gaze at Yingying any more. He lowered his head to go light the candle.

Yingying noticed Zhang after she heard the elder's words. She thought, "This young man is so handsome and talented. Is he walking here and there in the hall just to be near me?" Hongniang whispered to her, "Look at Zhang Sheng. I guess he didn't get much sleep last night; he must have been waiting to see you during the day." Yingying pretended to be angry, and said, "Don't talk nonsense!"

Zhang noticed Yingying and Hongiang were looking at him. He felt so happy and thought, "Yingying, can you feel my love for you?" At that time, the elder rose and declared, "The service is over. Madam and Miss Cui may return to their rooms now." "So soon?" Zhang could not get enough of Yingying. He dragged his feet as he left the hall.

"When can I see Yingying again? How can I be introduced to her?" Again, Zhang couldn't fall asleep.

3. Zhang Becoming a Hero and Saving Yingying

Zheng was worried sick wondering how to go further with Yingying. Meanwhile, something happened to the monastery.

Sun Feihu, a general in revolt, led rebels to rob civilians, burn their houses and even kill people. He learned that Mr. Cui's daughter was beautiful, so he wanted to take her as his wife. Sun sent his army to surround the monastery and demanded the elder surrender Yingying to him within three days. Otherwise, he would burn it down and slaughter all the monks.

Yingying was in her room thinking about what had happened over the past couple of days when her mother and the elder knocked on her door. She opened the door and Madam Cui started weeping, "My dear child, something terrible has happened. Sun Feihu, a rebel, has sent his troops to surround the monastery and has demanded to take you as his wife. What can we do?" Yingying was terrified after hearing her mother's words. She felt helpless. Both mother and daughter cried for some time. Then, Yingying said, "Mother, give me to the rebel troops. Otherwise, neither our family nor anyone else in the monastery can survive this." Madam Cui said, "How can I? You're my only daughter! How could I bear the thought of marrying you to a rebel?"

Yingying thought for a while and said, "Mother, then we can try another way. There are many people in the monastery. You and the elder go tell everyone that you will marry me to whoever drives away the rebels. Maybe someone will work out a solution."

"This might be the solution. At least it's better than marrying a rebel." Madam Cui and the elder hastened to the hall and declared, "If anyone can force the rebels to retreat, Madam Cui will marry Yingying to him!"

Upon hearing this, Zhang rose and said without hesitation, "I have an idea!" Madam Cui was happy to hear it and immediately asked, "What is your solution?" Zhang answered, "There are too many ears and mouths here. The elder and Madam Cui, let's discuss it in private."

Yingying had mixed feelings when she learned Zhang offered a solution. She thought, "I really hope Zhang can make it happen, but he is only a scholar. How can he defeat the rebels? Will he end up being captured by them? Ugh …" Tears came to her eyes again.

After they entered the room. Madam Cui and the elder hurried to ask, "What good solution do you have, Mr. Zhang? Please tell us." Zhang said calmly, "First of all, I need the elder to confront the rebel forces." The elder paled at the thought. He said, "I'm just a monk. How can I defeat these forces? Please ask someone else to do it."

Zhang smiled and said, "I'm not asking you to fight. I'm asking you to tell them that 'Miss Cui's father just passed away. She needs to do a religious service for three days for him. Please retreat for 15 kilometers. After three days, Miss Cui will go with you. Otherwise, she would rather die than go with you.' I think this will be enough for them to retreat for the moment." The elder did as Zhang told him and the rebels agreed to retreat and return after three days.

After that, the elder and Madam Cui asked Zhang, "What will we do in three days? Please tell us, Mr. Zhang." Zhang said confidently, "I have a classmate named Du Que. He is also known as 'General White Horse.' His army is stationed nearby. I'll write to him. He will definitely lead his men to help us." The elder and Madam Cui were delighted upon hearing this. "Considering the urgency of the matter, please write the letter now."

When Zhang finished the letter, the elder found the monastery's bravest monk to deliver it to General Du. Two days later, General Du and his troops came and defeated the rebels. Everyone was indebted to Zhang. Surely, Zhang was beaming with happiness. He thought, "I can finally be with Yingying. I couldn't be happier even if I became the Champion Graduate! When will Madam Cui set a date for our wedding? I wish time could go faster …."

4. The Fiancée Becoming Part of the Family

That day, Zhang dressed carefully and paced back and forth in his room. He thought, "Why has Madam Cui not summoned me? When will she marry Yingying to me?" Then Hongniang came for him. After they greeted each other, Zhang asked, "What can I do for you?" Hongniang replied, "You had the rebels retreated. Madam Cui asked me to invite you for dinner. Do you have time?"

Zhang answered without hesitation, "Of course, of course! I can go right now."

"He must have waited for this moment for a long time," Hongniang thought, then said, "Please make sure to come. I'll take my leave now."

Zhang was still worried. He went on to ask, "What will Madam Cui tell me during the dinner?"

"It's something you are thinking about right now. The marriage between you and Sister Yingying!" Hongniang said with a smile.

"I'm only a poor scholar, without money or status. Will Madam Cui marry Yingying to me for real?" Zhang asked with a heavy heart.

"Please rest assured. You saved everyone. Madam Cui and Miss Cui always keep their promises. She will consent to your marriage," she replied.

In the evening, Zhang went to Madam Cui's place where she received him warmly. She said, "Mr. Zhang defeated the rebels and saved the Cui family. We owe everything to you. Please, let me serve you some wine." Zhang said quickly, "I don't deserve it. How could I have you serve me wine?" Madam Cui insisted and served him. Then, she turned around and said to Hongniang, "Go and ask my daughter to come here. She needs to curtsy to Mr. Zhang." Zhang thought with excitement, "Madam Cui really keeps her word. She's going to marry Yingying to me."

Hongniang went to Yingying's room. She said, "Madam Cui asked you to see a gentleman."

Yingying thought for a while and said, "I'm not feeling well. I don't want to get up."

Hongniang smiled and said, "Don't you want to know who the gentleman is?"

"Who is he?" Yingying pretended to take no interest.

"It's Zhang Sheng! If you doesn't want to meet him, then so be it," Hongniang pretended to leave.

The moment she heard his name, Yingying rose and said, "Wait a moment. I'm feeling much better now. I will go with you."

Yingying walked along and thought, "Thanks to Zhang, our family was saved. I hope mother will keep her word and let Zhang and me be together."

"Sister, you are so beautiful today. Zhang is a lucky man!"

Hongniang whispered to Yingying.

"Don't talk that way!" Yingying said, as she pretended to be angry.

In the meeting room, the eyes of Zhang and Yingying met and quickly diverged.

Hongniang looked at the couple and murmured, "Well, the two were lovesick. They yearned for each other every day. Finally, they are happy today."

Yingying said to herself, "In the future, neither of us will be lovesick. We will always be together."

Hongniang was a bit worried. She whispered, "Marriage is an important event. Why has Madam Cui simply prepared a dinner instead of arranging a wedding banquet?"

Yingying thought for a while and said, "Mother is careful with money. Wedding banquets cost a lot of money. Zhang doesn't have much, so this is how it is."

Madam Cui took Yingying's hand and walked her to Zhang. Zhang was so happy and excited at the same time. Yingying tilted her head in shyness. They were waiting for Madam Cui to declare them married; however, Madam Cui said instead, "Yingying, curtsy to your elder brother."

"Brother, why brother? My mother changed her mind?" thought Yingying. She was taken by surprise and did not know how to respond.

"Call me brother? The old lady changed her mind?" Zhang was disheartened. "It must be because I don't have money or high status."

"Oh, Madam Cui changed her mind. Well, the two lovebirds have to suffer longer," Hongniang thought with a sigh.

Seeing the three standing there without any response, Madam Cui said, "Yingying, go and serve your brother some wine." Yingying walked to Zhang and poured the wine for him without saying anything.

Madam Cui said, "From now on, you will be brother and sister. Yingying, you may return to your room now." With tears welling up in her eyes, Yingying turned around and retreated to her room.

Zhang finished his wine in one gulp and said, "Madam, I would like to ask you a question. Days before, you said you would marry Yingying to whomever made the rebels retreat. Why did you break your promise today?" Madam Cui sat down and said slowly, "Mr. Zhang, indeed, you saved my entire family; however, when my husband was still alive, he already promised to marry Yingying to Zheng Heng, my nephew. So, I made you brother and sister. I will give you some money. You can find someone better to marry."

"Madam, I didn't save Yingying for money. I'm drunk and ask your permission to leave." Zhang's mind went blank. Madam Cui said, "In that case, I won't keep you long. Hongniang, help Zhang return to his room."

5. Music at Night

Supported by Hongniang, Zhang walked toward his room. Hongniang said, "Zhang, why didn't you hold back from drinking. You are so drunk."

Zhang was full of grievances. He suddenly knelt down and

shouted, "Hongniang, don't you know what has been on my mind? Because of Yingying, I lost my appetite for food and can't sleep. Finally, I thought this time I could marry Yingying, but your Madam went back on her word. I don't want to live any longer. I will end my life right here in front of you. Please tell Yingying what she means to me. I will go and hang myself now."

Hongniang felt angry and at the same time amused. "You are such a fool. Are you ending your life over such a minor obstacle? Don't worry. Let me find a way to help you."

"What do you have in mind? Go ahead and tell me!" Zhang said to Hongniang anxiously.

Hongniang thought for a while and said, "I've got it! Miss Cui likes to listen to *guqin* pieces. I remember you can play. When she and I go to burn incense today in the garden, I will give you a cue by coughing. After that, you can play *guqin* and see what Miss Cui says."

"Okay, we can give it a try." Zhang returned to his room and fell asleep embracing his *guqin*.

The moon rose, big and bright. Zhang was caressing the *guqin* in his room and said to himself, "*Guqin*, you have been with me for many years. I will count on you this evening. Allow me to play beautiful melodies for Yingying's ears, so that she can understand my feelings." A cough interrupted his thought.

"Here she comes." Zhang summoned his energy and began to play.

Yingying and Hongniang were burning incense when they heard the music. Yingying wondered, "Where is this music coming from? It's so touching, as if it were communicating someone's deepest feelings."

Hongniang said, "You stay here and enjoy the music. I will wait upon Madam Cui."

Then, Zhang began to play *A Male Phoenix Seeks His Mate*, a well-known piece. While playing, he sang, "I met a beautiful lady who is not to be forgotten after the first sight. I miss her wildly if I don't see her each day. The male phoenix is roaming around, just to look for his lady phoenix."

Yingying recognized the tune. "It must be Zhang. He is expressing his feelings using music." The scenes came back to Yingying: the time they first met; Zhang bravely offering to drive away the rebels; her mother refusing to fulfill her words. Tears rolled down her cheek.

Yingying said, in the direction the music was coming from, "Zhang Sheng, I understand your feelings."

The music stopped. Zhang said, "Yingying, do you really understand? Aren't you lying to trick me?"

Yingying wept, "Of course I understand. Don't hold hard feelings against me. My mother changed her mind. I couldn't do anything to help it …."

While they were talking, Hongniang ran over and said, "Sister, Madam Cui asked for you. We should go now." Yingying kept looking back as she made her way. The music resumed.

6. Hongniang Passing the Love Letter

Zhang fell sick and lethargically lay on his bed. Suddenly, there was a knock on the door.

"Who is it?" asked Zhang feebly.

"I'm a doctor specializing in curing lovesickness." Following a fit of laughter, Hongniang walked in.

Zhang gained some energy after he saw Hongniang. He asked, "How has your lady been the last few days?"

"Well," Hongniang said with a smile, "she is so lovesick, just like you. Before breakfast, she mentioned your name several hundred times."

Hearing her words, Zhang sat up and said, "This is a poem I wrote for her. Since she also misses me, could you please help me pass it to her?"

"Is it proper? I know her. She would be offended if a love poem were passed to her directly. She might simply tear the letter apart," Hongniang said reluctantly.

Zhang eagerly said, "You must help me. As long as I have the money, I will buy you a lot of gifts."

Hongniang was angered by his words and said, "Do you think that I'm helping you for money? I sympathize with you and think you and Miss Cui would make a great couple. That's why I'm trying to help you."

Zhang replied in a hurry, "May I have your sympathy and help again? If not, I won't go on living…."

Hongniang said, "Okay, rest assured. I will have the letter delivered to her."

Holding Zhang's letter, Hongniang thought, "How can I pass it to her. If I give it to her directly, she will be angry. I may leave it on the mirror. She will notice it when she uses the mirror."

Yingying went to look at herself in the mirror. She saw a letter and opened it. In the letter, the poem read, "I miss you more and more; I tried to play music for a distraction. In the beautiful spring, I am longing for a beautiful relationship. When love strikes, one shall not evade. Don't waste the night with beautiful moonlight; let's go appreciate the flowers under the moon." Yingying immediately understood it was about her and Zhang. She was also sure that Zhang wrote the letter.

Hongniang was waiting cautiously to see Yingying's reaction. First, Yingying blushed and then frowned. All of a sudden, she cried, "Hongniang, come here."

"Oh, no. She's mad at me." Hongniang made haste to approach her and said, "What's the matter, sister?"

Yingying said angrily, "What's the matter? Tell me, where is this letter from? I was the daughter of the Counselor-in-Chief. No one should write such a poem to me. I will tell my mother. Let's see how she will punish you!"

Hongniang understood that Yingying was pretending to be angry. She said indifferently, "Okay, I will show it to Madam Cui myself, and tell her Zhang wrote it…."

"No, no, Hongniang. I'm kidding you," Yingying said with a smile this time. "Tell me, how is Zhang doing lately?"

Hongniang said, "Zhang can neither sleep nor eat. He's become so thin. Day and night, he weeps while facing the direction of our place …."

"Ah, is he so seriously ill? Let's get a doctor for him," said

Yingying with concern. She added, "Hongniang, there is nothing unusual between Zhang and me. Mother asked us to be brother and sister. I care about him like a sister."

Hongniang laughed and said, "Who are you trying to fool? If you are brother and sister, how could Zhang fall ill like that?"

Yingying hastened to add, "My dear Hongniang, don't ever tell my mother that. Otherwise, it won't end nicely. How about I write a letter to Zhang? You go and tell him I consider him my elder brother and nothing more. Tell him not to write such poems to me any more, or I will let Mother know." With that, Yingying took up a piece of paper and a brush and began to write the letter.

7. Zhang Decoding Yingying's Poem

Hongniang went to see Zhang with Yingying's letter.

"Nice to see you. What did she say?" Zhang asked eagerly.

Hongniang said helplessly, "Zhang, you'd better be prepared. She got angry seeing the letter. She said she considers you an elder brother only and asked you not to write to her any more. I cannot do anything to help."

"Oh, how did this happen? What went wrong? Hongniang, you must help me!" Zhang, again, knelt down before Hongniang and cried while holding a corner of her dress.

Hongniang said, "Well, there is nothing I can do. This is the letter she wrote in reply. Go ahead and read it yourself."

Zhang wasted no time opening the letter. He saw a poem by Yingying, "In the west chamber, waiting for the moon to rise, a breeze pushed the door ajar. On the wall, shadows of the flowers were dancing. Has the lover come?" Zhang read it carefully. Suddenly, he said, "Hongniang, I'm so grateful to you! Yingying's words were a pretense. In her poem, she asked me to meet her tonight for a date!"

"How can you tell?" Hongniang asked in curiosity.

Zhang felt smug and said, "I'm a decoding expert. Take a look. The first line tells the time: when the moon rises. The second line implies she will keep the door open for me. The third and fourth lines mean she wants me to climb over the wall to meet her. Great! I will climb the wall now."

Hongniang said, "It's only noon."

"When will night fall?" Zhang waited anxiously for the sun to set and the moon to rise.

Hongniang returned to their room. She thought, "Miss Cui kept me in the dark and asked Zhang out through a poem. I won't tell her what I learned and wait to see what she is going to do." Then she said to Yingying, "Sister, the moon has risen. Let's go and burn incense in the garden." Gazing at the moon, Yingying said, "Today's moon is extraordinarily round. It's such a beautiful evening." Hongniang thought, "I think you, like Zhang, are eagerly waiting for the evening to come."

The two arrived at the garden. Yingying began burning incense. Hongniang sneaked to a corner and opened a side gate. She thought, "According to the poem, Zhang should enter through this gate. I'm wondering if he has come yet."

Zhang had long been waiting by the wall. He planned to climb over it after Yingying came. Suddenly, the side gate opened. "Yingying has opened the gate for me. She really is in love with me!" Zhang was wild with joy. He went through the gate and saw a beautiful figure. "Yingying!" Zhang embraced the beauty in no time.

"Let go of me, you beast! I'm Hongniang," the beauty gave out a cry.

Zhang found it was Hongniang. He hastened to apologize, "Sorry, I'm so sorry! I didn't have time to recognize you before I embraced you."

Hongniang smoothed her dress and said in a low voice, "What a troublemaker! Miss Cui is by the lake. Go and find her there."

Zhang walked to the lake and saw Yingying burning incense there. He slowly approached and held her in his arms. Yingying was startled and asked, "Who is it?"

"It's me, Zhang."

Yingying pushed him away and said angrily, "Zhang, who do you think I am? I'm burning incense here. What are you here for? You are an educated man. Don't you know that men and women should keep a proper distance from each other?" Then Yingying turned her back and shouted to Hongniang, "Hongniang, there's a thief. Let's leave now."

Hongniang realized Yingying was mad. She quickly came over and pretended to scold Zhang, "Zhang, I didn't realize you are such a person. Come over and kneel before Miss Cui to apologize, or we will tell Madam Cui about it. Then let's see what happens to you."

Seeing two angry women, Zhang's mind went blank. His face turned red and words failed him. He knelt down and apologized to Yingying.

Yingying said, "Zhang, my mother asked me to treat you like a brother. This time I will let it go. If anything similar happens again, I will tell my mother. Hongniang, let's go!"

Hongniang took Zhang's hand to help him stand up. She whispered, "You claimed to be a decoding expert. Your decoding didn't work well this time."

Zhang smiled bitterly and said, "Women's codes are so difficult to break. I won't try it again."

8. A Date under the Moonlight

Looking at herself in her room's mirror, Yingying was deep in thought.

"Sister, I heard from Madam Cui that Zhang is very ill. Many physicians came to treat him," said Hongniang.

"Really, is he so ill? Hongniang, go and take a look," Yingying said with concern.

Hongniang said, "It was all because you scolded him so harshly. I guess he was very disheartened this time."

Yingying rose up and said, "Well, Hongniang, I will write him a prescription. You can take it to him. He will recover after seeing it."

Hongniang said, "You're not a physician. How can you write a prescription? Moreover, things between you two have already been so awkward after last time. I don't want to be the messenger again."

"Nice Hongniang, please do help me this time. What if Zhang doesn't recover? Rest assured, my prescription will work," Yingying begged.

"Okay, this will be the last time I help you two. Give me the prescription," Hongniang said reluctantly.

Zhang was in bed thinking about Yingying's words. He felt helpless in winning her love. "Women are so fickle. It is impossible to understand them." At that time, Hongniang arrived.

"Zhang, are you feeling better?" she asked.

Zhang smiled bitterly and said, "How could I feel better? It's all because of you two."

Hongniang said with a sigh, "So many people have been lovesick. None of them wore down their health because of love. Here is the prescription Miss Cui wrote for you. Take a look to see if it is a cure."

"Prescription?" Zhang immediately sat up. He took the letter from Hongniang's hand and saw a poem, "Don't give certain things too much thought, it will be a waste of your talent. I intended to bring happiness to you, but I only caused you to suffer. I cannot tell you my feelings in explicit words and can only use the poem to send a message. This evening, please wait for me."

"Great!" Zhang stood up with a clap of his hands. "This evening, Yingying will come to me!"

"Are you sure? Are you decoding again?" Hongniang joked at Zhang.

"I must be right this time. Please rest assured," Zhang said excitedly. "Go back and tell her that I'm fully recovered and that I will tidy up my room."

The moon rose. Yingying said, "Hongniang, it's getting late. It's time for bed."

Hongniang said with a smile, "Time for bed? What about that fool? Are you tricking him again?"

"Which fool?" Yingying blushed.

"Don't pretend that you don't know," Hongniang pursed her lips and said, "I will go to see if Madam Cui is asleep. After she goes to bed, you can go to meet your sweetheart."

Yingying blushed and was speechless.

A moment later, Hongniang returned and said, "Miss, let's go now. Madam Cui is sleeping." Lowering her head, Yingying quietly walked toward Zhang's room with Hongniang, trying not to attract any attention.

In his room, Zhang was waiting anxiously. "Will Yingying come tonight? If she comes, I will be the happiest person in the world. Otherwise, I will be the most miserable person in this world. Love is torture." Then, he saw the shadow of people projected on the window. "It must be Yingying!" Zhang hurried to greet her.

"Zhang, kneel down to thank your matchmaker," Hongniang joked. "I brought Miss Cui to you."

Zhang quickly knelt down and said, "Thanks for your help Hongniang!" Yingying helped Zhang stand up. Zhang held her hand and gazed at her pretty face. He said, "Am I in a dream?" Yingying blushed and followed Zhang into his room. The two lovers were finally together.

9. Engagement and Imperial Civil Examination

Madam Cui had been watching Yingying closely these days. She found that there was something unusual about her. She was often lost in thought and sometimes would smile for no reason at all. Madam Cui had been told that Yingying and Hongniang went to the garden every evening to burn incense and they always returned late. "Is there something going on between her and Zhang?" Madam Cui grew worried. She said, "Go and find Hongniang. I need to ask her something."

Hongniang came to meet Madam Cui and saw her enraged face. "Hongniang, kneel down! Don't you know your wickedness?"

"No, I don't. I didn't do anything wrong," Hongniang raised her head, looking at Madam Cui.

"You are so stubborn. Spit it out, where do you take my daughter every evening? To meet Zhang? You'd better tell me the truth. Or I will beat you to death." With that, Madam Cui asked a servant to beat Hongniang.

After several strikes, Hongniang raised her hand and said, "Madam, stop beating me, please. I have something to say."

"Go ahead," Madam Cui said and signaled the servant to stop.

Hongniang said slowly, "Madam, Miss Cui was together with Zhang, but it was your fault."

"My fault?" Madam Cui was furious.

"Yes," Hongniang continued, "you promised that Zhang could marry Miss Cui after the retreat of the rebels, but you didn't keep your word and asked them to be brother and sister. This was your first mistake. After the retreat of the rebels, you should have kept Miss Cui away from Zhang; however, we still live here. Sooner or later, something was bound to happen between two consenting lovers. That was your second mistake. Now things have already happened. The best way is to give your consent to their marriage and marry Miss Cui to Zhang."

"We are from a noble family with a long history. How can Yingying marry a poor man like him?" Madam Cui shook her head.

"Madam, even though he is just a poor scholar now, he is smart and excels in his studies. One day, he will become the Champion Graduate and receive a good position in the government. It is not necessarily a bad thing if Miss Cui marries him. Moreover, the two have already been together. Miss Cui likes only Zhang. I'm afraid she won't marry anyone else." Hongniang tried to convince Madam Cui.

Madam Cui thought Hongniang's words made sense. She said with a sigh, "Ah, such a disobedient child. What she has done leaves me no other choice but to marry her to the poor man."

Madam Cui asked Hongniang to summon Yingying and Zhang, and then gave consent to their marriage on one condition: Zhang must leave immediately to take the imperial civil examination in the capital city. He could marry Yingying only after gaining a scholarly honor and an official rank. Zhang didn't want to part with Yingying, but in order to marry her, Zhang had to agree.

The next day, Yingying, Hongniang, Madam Cui and the elder came to see Zhang off.

Madam Cui said, "Zhang, I'm marrying my daughter to you. You must become the Champion Graduate. It is the least she deserves."

Zhang replied, "Mother, please rest assured. I won't let you down."

Hongniang poured some wine for Yingying. Yingying raised her cup. Before she could talk, tears were streaming down her face. "We have to part shortly after our engagement. You are leaving for the capital city and not sure of the return date. Zhang, whether you win the title of Champion Graduate or not, come back right after the examination."

Zhang also shed tears. He said, "Please rest assured. I will return as soon as I finish the examination. Please wait for good news here." He wiped away tears and mounted the horse. He kept turning back. Far as he went, he seemed to be able to see the figure of Yingying.

Just at that moment, the autumn wind swept by, causing the yellow leaves to drift through the air. A row of wild geese flew southwards.

10. A Happy Ending for the Lovers

Zhang was gone for half a year. Each and every day, Yingying missed him. "The examination should be finished by now. How did Zhang do in the exam? Why hasn't he come back yet? Has he fallen in love with another woman?"

Her thoughts were interrupted by Hongniang who hurriedly approached her. Hongniang said, "Miss, Zheng Heng, the nephew of Madam Cui, has come. The one who was engaged to you previously."

"Zheng Heng? Why has he come?" Yingying worried that

something might go wrong, "Go and see what he and my mother are talking about."

Hongniang went to Madam Cui's room. She found Zheng crying and asking Madam Cui why she didn't marry Yingying to him. Madam Cui was embarrassed and explained everything to him.

Zheng wiped his eyes and asked, "Aunt, did you say that Yingying is engaged to Zhang and that Zhang went to take the exam in the capital?"

Madam Cui replied, "Yes, it has been half a year. We don't know how he did in the exam."

Zheng said, "I just came from the capital. Zhang became the Champion Graduate. Mr. Wei, a minister, liked him and married his daughter to him. Everyone in the capital heard the news."

"Is it so?" Madam Cui was beyond angry. "I knew he is not a good person! He abandoned my daughter after everything. Nephew, I'm going to marry Yingying to you."

"Thank you, aunt! I promise to treat Yingying well," Zheng said with a smile.

Hongniang ran to Yingying's room and said, "Miss, something terrible is going to happen! Madam is marrying you to Zheng Heng!"

"How could that be possible? Mother has already given Zhang her consent," Yingying asked anxiously.

"Zheng said that Zhang Sheng received the title of Champion Graduate and married the daughter of Minister Wei. He is going to stay in the capital and leave us behind," Hongniang explained angrily.

"Is that so? Has he forgotten about us being together?" Yingying wept.

Despite Yingying's unwillingness, Madam Cui decided to marry her to Zheng. She ordered the servants to prepare the wedding banquet for them.

During the preparation, a voice passed through the gate, saying, "Mr. Zhang Sheng, governor of Hezhong Prefecture arriving!" Zhang walked into the monastery in high spirits. He knelt down in front of Madam Cui and said, "Mother, I received the title of Champion Graduate after the exam in the capital city. Now, I'm the governor of Hezhong. I'm here to invite you and Yingying to my home!"

Madam Cui said angrily, "Please rise, Mr. Governor. I heard that you already married the daughter of Minister Wei. Now I'm going to marry my daughter to Zheng Heng."

"The daughter of Minister Wei? Who told you that?" Seeing Hongniang was beside Madam Cui, Zhang asked her, "Hongniang, what's happened?"

"You dare ask me?" said Hongniang angrily. "Just tell me how your new wife is. Is she even prettier than my sister?"

"Oh, no. I don't have a wife. Who told you that?" Zhang asked anxiously.

"Zheng Heng, the nephew of Madam Cui told us. So, you haven't been married?" Hongniang asked.

"If I have married someone else, let me die a terrible death. Hongniang, do you believe me now?" Zhang said seriously.

"Yes, I believe you. How about you and I go to see Miss Cui

together? Let's confront Zheng to see if he lied," said Hongniang while looking into Zhang's eyes.

Yingying was crying in her room. Zhang approached her and said, "Yingying, Zheng Heng was lying. I didn't marry the daughter of Minister Wei." Hongniang added, "That's right. I believe Zhang. Let's go and ask Zheng Heng to see if he was telling the truth."

While they were talking, General Du Que came to congratulate Zhang, his friend. He said, "Zhang, I heard you were Champion Graduate and have become the governor of Hezhong. I'm here to congratulate you." Zhang was happy to see Du. He said, "General Du, you have arrived at the perfect time. You know what happened in the capital. You can prove that I haven't married the daughter of Minister Wei, can you not?"

"Minister Wei's daughter? Nothing like this has happened. I can prove that Zhang returned right after the exam to meet his fiancée," Du said firmly.

Hongniang said, "So, Zheng was lying. He is so evil. Where is he now?"

At that time, a servant reported, "Zheng Heng knew his lie wouldn't hold up and fled."

General Du was furious and wanted to send his men to capture him. Madam Cui tried to mediate, "Let him go. After all, he is my nephew. Please let him leave for my sake." Zhang and Yingying also pleaded for mercy for him. In the end, General Du didn't pursue Zheng.

At last, Zhang Sheng and Cui Yingying lived happily together. No one would ever separate them.

练习题 Reading exercises

一、选择题。Choose the correct answer.

1. 张生多大年纪？（   ）

    A. 十八岁   B. 十九岁

    C. 二十三岁   D. 三十岁

2. 张生为什么想住在普救寺？（   ）

    A. 他要去长安参加考试

    B. 他的父亲去世了

    C. 普救寺房租便宜

    D. 莺莺住在普救寺

3. 张生是怎么知道莺莺每天晚上都去花园烧香的？（   ）

    A. 长老告诉他的   B. 小和尚告诉他的

    C. 红娘告诉他的   D. 他自己发现的

4. 白马将军是谁？（   ）

    A. 孙飞虎   B. 杜确

    C. 张生   D. 郑恒

5. 张生从叛军手中救了莺莺一家，老夫人是怎么感谢他的？
（   ）

    A. 把红娘嫁给了张生

B. 把莺莺嫁给了张生

C. 让莺莺和张生结成兄妹

D. 给了张生很多钱

6. 红娘告诉张生，莺莺最喜欢做什么？（   ）

  A. 烧香   B. 摘花

  C. 听琴   D. 看月亮

7 红娘为什么要帮助张生和莺莺？（   ）

  A. 张生答应给她很多钱

  B. 莺莺求她帮助自己

  C. 她觉得张生和莺莺很合适

  D. 她喜欢郑恒

8. 张生是在什么季节离开莺莺去京城考试的？（   ）

  A. 春天   B. 夏天

  C. 秋天   D. 冬天

9 关于郑恒，下面哪个说法不是正确的？

  A. 他是老夫人的侄子   B. 他和莺莺订过婚

  C. 他撒谎骗了老夫人   D. 他被杜确抓走了

10 张生最后跟谁结婚了？

  A. 红娘   B. 莺莺

  C. 卫尚书的女儿   D. 杜确的女儿

二、判断题：请根据故事内容判断下列说法是否正确，如果正确请标"T"，不正确请标"F"。
Decide whether the following statements are true (T) or false (F).

1. 张生是唐朝一个准备去京城赶考的读书人。（　）
2. 红娘问张生的年龄和生日，还问张生有没有结婚。（　）
3. 老夫人宣布，谁能打退叛军，就把莺莺嫁给谁。（　）
4. 张生出寺与孙飞虎拼命，救了莺莺。（　）
5. 莺莺反悔，不愿意嫁给张生，因为她已经跟郑恒订婚了。（　）
6. 张生翻过墙，见到了莺莺。（　）
7. 红娘帮张生传递情书，因为张生答应送她礼物。（　）
8. 老夫人要张生取得功名后才能和莺莺结婚。（　）
9. 张生去京城考试，得了第一名。（　）
10. 张生娶了卫尚书的女儿。（　）

三、选择填空。Choose the appropriate words to fill in the parentheses.

1.在普救寺里，张生这里看看，那里看看，（　　）到一个小花园，突然发现一位姑娘正在（　　）花。这位姑娘（　　）起来十八九岁，长得非常漂亮。张生（　　）了一惊，心想："世界上怎么会有这么美丽的姑娘？难道是天上的仙女？"这时又来了一个丫鬟（　　）的小姑娘，也非常漂亮，但是一（　　）眼两位姑娘都离开了花园。

A.摘　　　B.吃　　　C.看

D.转　　　E.走　　　F.打扮

2.当张生正在（　　）怎么和莺莺更进一步的时候，寺庙出事了。一个叫孙飞虎的将军（　　），到处杀人放火，（　　）老百姓。他听说崔相国的女儿非常漂亮，想抢来做自己的妻子，于是（　　）了军队（　　）了寺庙，要求寺庙长老三天之内把莺莺交给他，否则就把寺庙（　　）掉，把和尚们都杀光。

A.抢劫　　B.包围　　C.造反

D.烧　　　E.发愁　　F.派

3.红娘给莺莺倒上一杯酒，莺莺举起（　　），还没说话，已经是泪流满面："你我刚刚订婚就要分别。你去（　　），不知道什么时候才能回来。张生，不管这次能不能考中（　　），考完之后就快回来。"张生也流下了眼泪："你放心，考完我马上就回来，你在家等我的好（　　）。"哭完之后，张生骑上马，一步几回头地向前走了。张生走出去很远，似乎还可以看到莺莺的（　　）。

A.京城　　B.消息　　C.状元

D.酒杯　　E.影子

四、请根据故事的内容给下列句子排列顺序。
Put the following statements in order according to the story.

A. 孙飞虎派兵围住了普救寺，要抢莺莺做妻子。

B. 张生被莺莺拒绝后，生病了。

C. 张生中了状元，娶了莺莺。

D. 张生去京城参加考试，路过河中府，在普救寺住下。

E. 张生弹《凤求凰》，让莺莺知道了自己的心事。

F. 老夫人知道张生和莺莺的事以后，气得要打红娘。

G. 张生请杜将军派兵前来解围，救了莺莺。

五、思考题。Answer the following questions according to the story.

1. 老夫人为什么不愿意把莺莺嫁给张生？

2. 莺莺第一次和张生约会为什么要翻脸？

3. 红娘是怎样的一个人？

练习题答案 Keys to the exercises

一、选择题
    1. C   2. D   3. B   4. B   5. C
    6. C   7. C   8. C   9. D   10. B

二、判断题：请根据故事内容判断下列说法是否正确，如果正确请标"T"，不正确请标"F"
    1. T   2. F   3. T   4. F   5. F
    6. F   7. F   8. T   9. T   10. F

三、选择填空
    1. E   A   C   B   F   D
    2. E   C   A   F   B   D
    3. D   A   C   B   E

四、请根据故事内容给下列句子排列顺序
    D—A—G—E—B—F—C

五、思考题
    （答案略）

词汇表
Vocabulary List

报告	v.	bàogào	report
背影	n.	bèiyǐng	figure
毕竟	adv.	bìjìng	after all
表达	v.	biǎodá	express, convey
不慌不忙		bùhuāng-bùmáng	unhurriedly
才华	n.	cáihuá	talent
藏	v.	cáng	hide
沉	v.	chén	sink, plummet
吃惊	v.	chījīng	be surprised
传	v.	chuán	pass, transmit
答应	v.	dāying	promise, agree
大殿	n.	dàdiàn	hall
大人	n.	dàren	lord
大雁	n.	dàyàn	wild goose
弹琴		tán qín	play instrument
祷告	v.	dǎogào	pray
盯	v.	dīng	stare at
订婚	v.	dìnghūn	be engaged to
逗	v.	dòu	tease, trick
发愁	v.	fāchóu	worry, be anxious
法事	n.	fǎshì	religious service
翻脸	v.	fānliǎn	fall out with sb.
反悔	v.	fǎnhuǐ	go back on one's word, pull back
房租	n.	fángzū	rent
愤怒	adj.	fènnù	indignant
凤求凰		Fèng Qiú Huáng	*A Male Phoenix Seeks His Mate* is a *guqin* piece written during the Han Dynasty (206 BC-AD 220). It tells the story of two lovers who eloped. Phoenix is the legendary bird, and 凤 refers to the male phoenix while 凰 refers to the female one.
扶	v.	fú	support

福气	n.	fúqi	luck, blessing
府尹	n.	fǔyǐn	prefecture governor
负	v.	fù	fail to live up to, disappoint
尴尬	adj.	gāngà	awkward, embarrassed
赶紧	adv.	gǎnjǐn	hurriedly, hastily
告	v.	gào	tell, complain, report
告辞	v.	gàocí	bid farewell
功名	n.	gōngmíng	scholarly honor and official rank
姑姑		gūgu	aunt (father's sister)
观察	v.	guānchá	observe, watch
贵族	n.	guìzú	nobility
跪	v.	guì	kneel
果然	adv.	guǒrán	as expected, really
含	v.	hán	bear, hold in the mouth
喝醉		hēzuì	get drunk
和尚	n.	héshang	Buddhist monk
湖边	n.	hú biān	lakeside
花丛	n.	huācóng	flowers in clusters
花园	n.	huāyuán	garden
哗啦啦	onom.	huālālā	crash, rustle
坏蛋	n.	huàidàn	scoundrel, rascal
欢喜	adj.	huānxǐ	joyful, happy
婚礼	n.	hūnlǐ	wedding ceremony
婚宴	n.	hūnyàn	wedding banquet
纪念	v.	jìniàn	commemorate
家伙	n.	jiāhuo	fellow, guy
假装	v.	jiǎzhuāng	pretend
嫁	v.	jià	marry (a husband)
将军	n.	jiāngjūn	general
角落	n.	jiǎoluò	corner
教训	v.	jiàoxùn	admonish, lecture somebody
姐夫	n.	jiěfu	brother-in-law (elder sister's husband)
解围	v.	jiěwéi	lift a siege, get somebody out of a fix
紧急	adj.	jǐnjí	urgent
京城	n.	jīngchéng	capital (of a country)

眷属	n.	juànshǔ	husband and wife
军队	n.	jūnduì	army, troops
科举	n.	kējǔ	imperial civil examination
狂喜	adj.	kuángxǐ	wild with joy
凉	adj.	liáng	cold
亮	v.	liàng	shine, lighten
灵柩	n.	língjiù	coffin
瞒	v.	mán	conceal something
谜语	n.	míyǔ	riddle
面子	n.	miànzi	face, reputation
灭	v.	miè	go out
默默	adj.	mòmò	quiet, silent
男女授受不亲		nánnǚ shòushòu bù qīn	Men and women should keep a proper distance from each other. This was the norm in ancient China. It was forbidden for men and women to have any body contact or conversations or to pass things to each other.
闹	v.	nào	make a scene
念经	v.	niànjīng	chant Buddhist scriptures
扭	v.	niǔ	turn around
派	v.	pài	send, dispatch
盼	v.	pàn	long for, expect
叛军	n.	pànjūn	rebel forces
抛弃	v.	pāoqì	abandon, desert
撇嘴	v.	piězuǐ	purse one's lips
拼命	v.	pīnmìng	risk one's life, do something with all one's might
墙	n.	qiáng	wall
抢	v.	qiǎng	rush to
抢劫	v.	qiǎngjié	rob
亲自	adv.	qīnzì	in person
禽兽	n.	qínshòu	beast, dirty swine
倾诉	v.	qīngsù	pour out (one's heart, troubles, worries, etc.)
曲子	n.	qǔzi	tune
娶	v.	qǔ	marry (a wife)

去世	v.	qùshì	pass away
惹	v.	rě	cause, offend
入迷	v.	rùmí	be fascinated, be lost in
撒谎	v.	sāhuǎng	lie
傻瓜	n.	shǎguā	fool
上吊	v.	shàngdiào	hang oneself
烧	v.	shāo	burn
烧香	v.	shāoxiāng	burn incense
舍不得	v.	shěbude	loathe to part with
诗	n.	shī	poem
世世代代		shìshìdàidài	generations
帅气	adj.	shuàiqì	handsome
说情	v.	shuōqíng	plead for mercy for sb.
思念	v.	sīniàn	miss
撕	v.	sī	tear
寺庙	n.	sìmiào	temple, monastery
算数	v.	suànshù	count, hold
叹气	v.	tànqì	sigh
唐朝	n.	Tángcháo	the Tang Dynasty (618-907)
特意	adv.	tèyì	on purpose
天界	n.	tiānjiè	realm of heaven
偷偷	adv.	tōutōu	stealthily
透	adj.	tòu	clear, through
退兵	v.	tuìbīng	retreat
委屈	n.	wěiqu	grievance
无奈	v.	wúnài	resign oneself to
无所谓		wúsuǒwèi	be indifferent
西厢	n.	xīxiāng	west chamber
瞎	adv.	xiā	foolishly, blindly, groundlessly
吓坏	v.	xiàhuài	be terrified
仙女	n.	xiānnǚ	fairy
相国	n.	xiàngguó	Counselor-in-Chief
相思病	n.	xiāngsībìng	lovesickness
宣布	v.	xuānbù	announce, declare
寻找	v.	xúnzhǎo	look for

丫鬟	n.	yāhuan	maid
眼泪	n.	yǎnlèi	tear
宴席	n.	yànxí	banquet
药方	n.	yàofāng	prescription
夜	n.	yè	night
邮差	n.	yóuchāi	mailman
有情人	n.	yǒuqíngrén	lover
原诗		yuánshī	original poem
原文		yuánwén	original lyrics
怨	v.	yuàn	blame
约	v.	yuē	make an appointment
造反	v.	zàofǎn	rebel
摘	v.	zhāi	pluck, pick
长老	n.	zhǎnglǎo	elder
折磨	v.	zhémó	torture
整理	v.	zhěnglǐ	tidy
整整齐齐	adv.	zhěngzhěngqíqí	neatly
侄子	n.	zhízi	nephew (the son of one's brother)
治	v.	zhì	cure, treat
皱眉	v.	zhòuméi	frown
炷	m.w.	zhù	(for sticks of incense)
抓	v.	zhuā	catch
专家	n.	zhuānjiā	expert
转身	v.	zhuǎnshēn	turn around
装作	v.	zhuāngzuò	pretend
状元	n.	zhuàngyuan	Champion Graduate, title conferred to the one who placed first in the highest imperial civil examination
自言自语		zìyán-zìyǔ	talk to oneself
嘴硬	adj.	zuǐyìng	stubborn and reluctant to admit mistakes or defeats

项目策划：刘小琳　韩　颖
责任编辑：刘小琳
英文翻译：张　乐
英文编辑：韩芙芸
英文审定：James Hutchison［加］ 黄长奇
插图绘制：千秋叶工作室
设计指导：isles studio
设计制作：isles studio

图书在版编目（CIP）数据

西厢记：汉、英 / 王帅改编. — 北京：华语教学出版社，2017
（"彩虹桥"汉语分级读物. 4级：1000词）
ISBN 978-7-5138-1246-7

Ⅰ. ①西… Ⅱ. ①王… Ⅲ. ①汉语－对外汉语教学－语言读物 Ⅳ. ① H195.5

中国版本图书馆 CIP 数据核字（2016）第 165612 号

西厢记

王　帅　改编
张　乐　翻译

＊

©华语教学出版社有限责任公司
华语教学出版社有限责任公司出版
（中国北京百万庄大街24号　邮政编码 100037）
电话: (86)10-68320585　68997826
传真: (86)10-68997826　68326333
网址：www.sinolingua.com.cn
电子信箱：hyjx@sinolingua.com.cn
北京虎彩文化传播有限公司印刷
2017年（32开）第 1 版
2023 年第 1 版第 3 次印刷
（汉英）
ISBN 978-7-5138-1246-7
002900